Looking for the Goodness of God

Hi! Thanks for joining me as we journey together through the 40 Days of Grace.

Our journey begins in the book of Romans, which is actually a letter written by a man named Paul, and he wrote the letter to a church plant in Rome, a church plant similar to Skyline. He really wanted to visit them, and get to know them, but just in case he couldn't, he wrote them this letter. And what a letter! After telling them a little bit about himself he gets right down to business. He simply says, "I'm not ashamed of the Gospel..." (Romans 1:16-17)

If you're anything like the Romans, you're thinking, "Well, why are you saying that? What do you mean you're not ashamed of the Gospel?" Here's a good way to think it through...

Think about the quality of something you really value...that you're really proud of. Say, for example, it's your car. It's got a fast engine – can go a quarter of a mile in under 4 seconds. It has polished alloy hubcaps, a sleek European design, large 16-inch tires, and a paint job to die for. You are definitely not ashamed of that car! Well, that's the feeling Paul was going for when he said he wasn't "ashamed of the Gospel"

Then he tells them WHY he's not ashamed. It's quite extraordinary! He says he isn't ashamed because "it's the power of God!" – Imagine that! The Gospel is THE POWER of God! And not only that, "it's the power of God for the salvation of every single person who believes." WOW! What a way to grab their attention, huh? Power! Power to save - anyone, to change – anyone. Power to make someone brand new – anyone who believes.

Ok, so what would the Romans need to be saved from? If you asked, trust me, they asked too. And what's cool about the Romans letter is that Paul makes statements that makes the Romans ask questions, and then he answers their questions in a way that makes them ask more questions! As you read you'll find yourself caught up in all of these questions and answers – you might even have the same question the Romans did.

One important thing I need to tell you. There were both Jews and Gentiles living in Rome at the time. We know this because the verse goes on to say, "first for the Jew, and then for the Gentile." So some of the questions came from Jews. They lived under a Jewish law and asked questions based on that way of thinking. And some of the questions came from Gentiles, who didn't live by any law, and they had their own way of thinking. That should make it easier for you to understand why Paul wrote a certain way at certain times.

Keep reading!

It says, "for in the Gospel a righteousness from God

is revealed, a righteousness that's by faith." So…what's righteousness? Very simply – it's GOODNESS – it's perfect goodness. God is perfect goodness. That's his character – it's a perfect character. It means he knows the right thing to do…all the time, and he does the right thing…all the time, every time.

This week we're going to see just how good God is, and you'll be amazed at his qualities, which made Paul begin his letter, "I'm not ashamed."

Ok…so…he's not finished yet! The last thing he says is, " it is by faith, from first to last, just as it is written, the righteous will live by faith.

Are you asking the same questions the Romans are asking?

WHAT IN THE WORLD DOES THAT MEAN?

Welcome to the 40 Days of Grace! Let's find out together.

*Note for the rest of the series:

During this series, get rid of the words, "I ought to…" or "I should…" As we journey together we want to find out things as they ARE. We're not going to read to find out what we should be doing, we're reading to find out what is actually true.

List the things God would do in your life if he were truly good?

Do you take it for granted that God is good or have you seen his goodness? Where?

What in your life can you say you're not ashamed of? Why?

Is God 100% Pleased With Me?

Today, as we continue in our journey, I'd like you to do an exercise for me. I'd like you to answer this question:

Is God 100% pleased with you? Yes or no?

If yes, tell me why.

If no, tell me why not.

Grace Starts With God Being Angry

The wrath of God is being revealed from heaven against all the godlessness and wickedness of men who suppress the truth by their wickedness, since what may be known about God is plain to them, because God has made it plain to them. For since the creation of the world God's invisible qualities — his eternal power and divine nature — have been clearly seen, being understood from what has been made, so that men are without excuse.

Romans 1:18-20

A couple of days ago we were left with a statement from Paul that, frankly, left us as perplexed as the Romans were. We're trying to find out about this "righteousness" of God...this GOODNESS, and then he says that the righteous shall live by faith. We're SO ready for him to explain that. Instead, he talks about the wrath of God! Wait a minute! Where did that come from? Weren't we just talking about how good God is? What does God's wrath have to do with his goodness? Do I even want to know?

So...here's what he says.

"The wrath of God is being revealed from heaven against all the godlessness and wickedness of men who suppress the truth by their wickedness." (Romans 1:18-20)

5

Wrath means ANGER IN ACTION. It means that God's furious! Who is he furious with? Well...one of the very first things we learn about a "righteous character" is that it reacts to protect the weak. It reacts against wickedness. If someone is truly righteous...has good character...has perfectly righteous character, they react to people being hurt. They react to relationships being destroyed. They react to children who are being abused, to the innocent being taken advantage of. Someone with good character doesn't just walk by or just look the other way. That person does something about it, because a righteous person protects against the wicked. So...Paul says as strongly as he can that God's wrath...his anger...is being revealed from heaven...against people who do that!

So...here's what we've learned so far...God's really good, SO good he will protect the weak...the innocent...at all costs!

And then Paul says, here's what we know. We KNOW that there's truth out there. He doesn't say that we have to go searching for the truth. He actually says we "suppress the truth."

Picture this. Picture that you're in a swimming pool...you have a big beach ball with you, and you're trying to get the beach ball to go underneath the water. What happens? Yes! The ball keeps trying to come back to the surface. And as soon as you let go of the ball, that's exactly what it does!

That's' God's perspective! The truth is here, but we push it down all the time. We know what's right. We know what's good, but we push that down. We suppress that. And God's wrath is against that, too!

Wait! What truth? God's angry because I push down the truth...where would I see it? Where would I find it?

6

Well...He says that all of us see it...we're all accountable for it...it's all around us...here it is..."since what may be known about God is plain to them, because God has MADE it plain to them" WHERE?! WHERE HAS GOD MADE IT PLAIN TO ME?! WHERE WOULD I SEE WHAT'S TRUE?!

"For since the creation of the world God's invisible qualities, his eternal power and divine nature, have been clearly seen, being understood from what has been made known, so that men are without excuse." God's creation shows us that God is all powerful, that he loves beauty, that he loves order, that he's an AMAZING GENIUS! You see that all through creation. You just look at the stars and how huge and vast that night sky is, and how many things there are just sitting there...some we haven't even seen yet! Isn't it amazing that the male penguins in the South Pole will stand for three months just rotating and warming an egg until it's born? Who thought that up?

Here's the truth...

The truth is that there is no one...NO ONE on the face of this earth, no who has ever been born, who doesn't know, who hasn't seen that there is a God! As he says...we have NO EXCUSE.

Right now...in this moment...just think. Is there anything that you know is true, but you suppress it? Are your relationships with other people, or with your husband, or wife, falling apart because you just didn't know the truth, or because you knew the truth, you suppressed it, and you went in a different direction?

What's the truth? If I choose not to believe there is a God does that mean he does not exist? What does the universe including the earth, animals, plants and microbiology tell you about God?

The Slide of Sin

Romans 1:20-32

We know the truth. We have no excuse. Everything that we notice throughout the day – everything exquisite and beautiful – it all screams out – "GOD MADE ME! THERE IS A GOD!

So…How are we dealing with what we already know? Romans 1:21 says, "For although they knew God, they neither glorified him as God nor gave thanks to him, but their thinking became futile and their foolish hearts were darkened. Although they claimed to be wise, they became fools and exchanged the glory of the immortal God for images made to look like mortal man and birds and animals and reptiles. Therefore God gave them over…" I call this "The Slide of Sin" – it's what we do with what we already know… it's what we do with the truth…we slide away.

Here's the pattern…

We do interact with God. Remember – we know he's there by what we see – THAT'S INTERACTION! Then, we deny what we know to be true – we suppress the truth. And we've gotten pretty good at this since we've been doing it awhile. You remember. Mom said, "No cookies before dinner." What it looks like in our minds is, "She didn't really mean that." OR "My sister got one, why can't I?" OR "I can give you a very good reason why I should have that cookie, mom!" The list goes on and on because we're good at thinking up reasons why we need and should have that cookie! Somewhere in all of those reasons, the truth gets lost – pushed down. And then…the truth is not bothering us anymore.

What happens next?

Since we're not remembering the truth, we're thinking up some lies. "Mom never lets me have cookies." OR "Mom loves my sister more than me." Mom becomes the enemy. There's NO WAY we're thanking her for even making the cookies. We don't even remember a time, EVER, when mom even gave us a cookie. It gets pretty ridiculous from there on. So, the next step is that we're not thankful for what we have – what God gives us. We never say, "Wow, God was really good to give me that sunset…this marriage …this car…this job…

What would happen if we woke up every morning and said, "Wow, God, thanks for everything you created! Thanks for giving me life! Thanks for this JOB! I'm thinking that would really change the way we look at our jobs, don't you think?

The opposite is suppressing the truth. "Man, this job really stinks! My boss is too bossy, my coworkers don't mind their own business…" And THAT affects how we feel about our jobs, too.

Here's what's happening with our thinking.

First, our minds get messed up. We don't think right.

9

We don't see things as they really are. The truth becomes lies. When that happens, our hearts become darkened. It's like a cloud – it passes over our hearts. We can't relate to God, to each other. We close off our hearts…and we hide.

The next thing that happens is that we start worshipping or admiring or glorifying or pursuing other things. We look for OTHER things to provide what we need, or think we need – sometimes really awful things – instead of GOD – who has   AL-READY provided what we need.

The last step in our thinking is the scariest step of all. You read it earlier – it said – "GOD GAVE THEM OVER…"

Those are really scary words! The worse thing that God could ever do is to give you exactly what you want. What if God left you alone to act on your impulses, wants, desires? No one to say "no" or "that is not wise" or "you better not trust yourself on this one"? Keep going…

It says, "God gave them over to the desires of their hearts…" Later on, in verse 28 it says, "Furthermore, since they didn't think it was worthwhile to retain the knowledge of God, he gave them over to a depraved mind, to do what ought not to be done."

Left to themselves, here's what they'd become: "They had become filled with every kind of wickedness, evil, greed and depravity. They're full of envy, murder, strife, deceit and malice. They are gossips, slanderers, God-haters, insolent, arrogant and boastful; they invent ways of doing evil; they disobey their parents; they are senseless, faithless, heartless, ruthless. Although they know God's righteous decree that those who do such things deserve death, they not only continue to do these very things but also approve of those who practice them."

And it all started out by simply suppressing the truth – and we slide from there – right into sin. We don't think right. We don't relate with each other right. We don't relate to God right. Everything we go after – everything we pursue – is empty, futile, just like the verse says.

The reality is that the slide of sin crashes head-on into the truth. And the truth is that THE WORSE THING THAT COULD EVER HAPPEN IS THAT GOD GIVES US OVER TO WHAT WE WANT...and God's wrath will be poured out.

Have you found that the first lie makes the second lie easier? Do you find yourself doing things that at one time in your life you promised you would never do? Why?

How do we go from "I love you" to "I hate you"? How do we go from "I believe stealing is wrong" to "it is understandable why I take what I do"?

Can you track a sin in your life that has hurt you or the ones you love? How did it get started? What did you stop being thankful for? Go back to that point and start all over by being thankful and obeying God one step at a time.

Moralist/Religious

Romans 2:1-28

What are your questions? What are you thinking? Write them down!

Maybe you read the LIST from yesterday, the LIST at the end of chapter 1, and you've come to the conclusion that…"NO WAY! That's not me…I'm really a good person inside…I'm really trying to do the right thing." You're not alone. It's what the people in Rome were thinking, too. And Paul knew that.

So in chapter 2 we'll take a look at what he says about those of us who are really trying our best. "You, therefore, have no excuse, you who pass judgment on someone else…" (Romans 2:1)

Wait…pass judgment…What do you mean? Who's passing judgment?

What does it mean to pass judgment on someone else? It means to say, "Ok, well, I'm doing better than that person…especially if I compare myself to THAT LIST!" That's passing judgment. You're basing your righteousness, your goodness, your standing with God or the universe or however you look at it, on… "Ok…

as I look around the world, as I look around at other people, I think I'm doing a little bit better job than what they're doing...I mean, really, the important things are...I haven't murdered anybody. I have never really set out to hurt anybody. I don't steal. Whatever the list is...YOU ARE DOING MUCH BETTER THAN THAT!

And Paul has the most amazing response to that... He says, "...at whatever point you judge the other, you are condemning yourself because you pass judgment. You who pass judgment do the same things!"

Here's the deal...Make up your own rules. Make up your own laws. And then say, "Ok, if I and everyone else keep these rules, keep these laws, then we'll be righteous, and then I'll be fine and this person and that person get to go to heaven, and that person is considered ok"...The Bible says that whatever LIST you create, you'll end up breaking...and that's why God's righteousness is not based on THE LIST.

A little bit later, in verse 4, it says, "...or do you show contempt for the riches of his kindness, tolerance and patience, not realizing that it's God's kindness that leads you toward repentance."

The bottom line is, and we'll see the BIG picture in just a bit, it's going to be God's kindness that leads us toward him...it is not our own efforts...THERE IS NO LIST THAT'S GOOD ENOUGH!

Maybe you have found truth. In Rom 3:18 God says maybe you boast because you call yourself a Jew. The Jews were and are God's chosen people. God wanted to show the whole world who he was by developing a special relationship with one nation. He chose Abraham, remember that name he will come up again several times on our journey. God made some huge promises to Abraham about building a nation from his family and wanting to bless the whole world through that nation. The nation is the Jewish nation. Yes, the very ones that live in Israel and all around the world today. They were given God's Word and a way to live called the law. This is called the Old Testament. They had a huge advantage. And by the time Paul wrote this it was some 3000 years later. The Jews believed that because of their religion, heritage and special knowledge they were righteous. They were convinced they had found the right religion, they had found the truth. And they were right.

How about you? What religion have you found? What do you know about right and wrong? Is your claim to being right that you're Baptist, Catholic, Lutheran, Muslim, Hindu, Christian? For the Jew who did have the truth God said that knowing the truth, teaching others the truth, doing the rituals or following the works don't help or prove anything about your character.

The question is, "How do you live?" Do you live out what you say you believe?

Is your heart right like God's heart?

What religion or set of teachings do you think are true?

How well do you live by your religion, beliefs?

Whole World

We've been searching for righteousness...goodness. Yesterday we found out that there is no righteousness in any list that anyone could ever create. No list will ever be enough. Even if you find the right religion do you live by those beliefs?

So where can we find it?

Well...we found out that we can see righteousness in the Gospel, where we find out about God's character. It's where we find out just how good he is. It's also where we found out about his wrath – his anger – at just how "not good" WE are! Who is he angry with? Who is his wrath against?

- His wrath is against the person who shakes his fist at God. Who says, "I'm not interested in anything you have to say or give."

- His wrath is against the person who judges others - sets his own standard. He decides what's important, points to another and says, "Thank God I'm not like that - I don't do those things."

15

- His wrath is against the person who declares himself religious...declares himself to know the truth. "I'm ok. I'm acceptable because of what I know." But then...they really don't practice it at all.

Well...none of those are me, so he must not be angry at me, right? Paul summarizes it all up with some incredibly strong words...I mean really powerful words... about EACH ONE OF US. Yes, US!

So if you didn't find yourself in any of the other types of people we talked about...well, frankly, you're not off the hook. Today you're going to find YOURSELF.

"What shall we conclude then? Are we any better? Not at all! We have already made the charge that Jews and gentiles alike are all under sin. As it is written: There is no one righteous, not even one. There is no one who understands, no one who seeks God." Did you catch the words? NO ONE!

Have there been times in your life when you've said, "I want to know God. I just desire God. I've had this empty place in my life and I've been looking for God." Strong words... BUT GOD DOESN'T AGREE WITH YOU! He says that NO ONE actually looks for a righteous one. NO ONE actually looks for a God who has the character that he has. As a matter of fact, it's JUST THE OPPOSITE! Paul says that when we see God, "All have turned away, they have together become worthless; there is no one who does good, not even one."

Worthless! It sounds harsh. And so do the graphic terms he uses to describe it all. I mean, he's really trying to get a point across here! He talks about their throats...their tongues...their lips and mouths...their feet. It's not too different from what we do when we're really angry at someone! And then he wraps it up – "there is no fear of God before their eyes."

Here's the thing. As we look at our lives, the way we live our lives, we are so use to sin – so use to being a part of it – that when a person sins just a little less than someone else, we think they're good! But really, looking at who God is, do we fear God enough to live the way he says?

Well...Paul says, really, NO ONE DOES.

And he leaves us with this really strong statement that kind of settles the matter, "Now we know that whatever the law says, it says to those who are under the law, so that every mouth may be silenced and the whole world held accountable to God."

What is your plan for getting into heaven?

Did you get it from *People Magazine, Sports Illustrated,* Sunday School, Grandma, favorite professor, MTV, CNN, self realization, what someone told you about the Bible?

According to what we have learned so far does God agree with your plan?

Can I Improve My Standing With God?

Therefore no one will be declared
righteous in his sight by observing
the law; rather, through the law we
become conscious of sin.
Romans 3:20

Let's review for just a moment…
We know who God is because of and through creation and his word. We know who God is through our own consciences. We know that even though we know who God is, we don't…CAN"T…keep the law. We know that   because we can't keep the law we're held accountable – we have to answer to – God.

So…if God is truly a good God, a righteous God, then what we have to answer to is GOODNESS…RIGHTEOUSNESS. And we have to answer to God because God's character protects the innocent. He wants to protect the innocent against those who do wrong.

Well, that about sums it up so far.

Ok, so, Paul makes this amazing statement. He says, "Therefore no one will be declared righteous in his sight by observing the law; rather, through the law we become conscious of sin."

Now, this should go against everything that you've

ever been taught...everything you've ever thought
since you were little. Here's the idea we've always
believed, always been taught. "The thing that God really cares about is my behavior. If I just change my behavior, then maybe I'll make it...maybe I'll be ok. God
will be happy with me." Some of us have learned that
when we do wrong...God's sad. When we do right
God's happy...because all he cares about is our
behavior.

But what Paul's saying is that no one's character will
ever be changed by observing the law. If you have a
selfish character, just because you go around doing a
few things right now and then, doesn't make you an
unselfish person. If you have a gossiping nature, just
because you stop gossiping doesn't mean that you
don't have a gossiping nature. It really is what you
ARE.

The law is like a giant mirror. When God tells us
what we should and shouldn't do, when he tells us
what's good and what's bad...the mirror shows us,
"Hey, wow, that's not me...that's not where I am."
That's what Paul means when he says "the law makes
us conscious of sin."

We're still at the beginning of this journey, and as we
begin this journey...and we cannot begin without doing this...the most important thing we can do
is...WE'VE GOT TO QUIT TRYING...we've got to quit
trying to become righteous. Quit! Give it up! "Trying"
won't work. The idea that I can please God or become
pleasing to God by changing my behavior is faulty. He
does not operate that way. It's a faulty system. Any
system we choose will simply not work. Not one
person's character has ever changed because he kept a
few rules or almost all the rules. God will not look the

other way…he will not ignore who we really are… just because we change our behavior.

What kind of pressure comes with trying to become pleasing to our parents, family, friends, spouses, even ourselves with our behavior?

What have you been trying to do right so God would bless you?

What kind of pressure comes with trying to please God with our behavior?

What would your life look like if you gave up on trying to get on God's good side?

God's Goodness May Be Too Good To Be True

Romans 3:21-24

Ok…

In searching for God's righteousness we now understand that a righteousness from God is revealed in the Gospel, and that God's character is good. Now we're really going to look at God's character and see just HOW GOOD HE IS.

His identity is good…GOOD is who he is! He holds those who hurt others, those whose identity is bad character…sinful character…he holds them accountable for what they do and who they are. And it has been made really clear that no one's identity can ever be changed because he acted differently for awhile. God does not look at us differently because we changed our behavior. He won't declare us righteous, because we, in fact, ARE NOT RIGHTEOUS. He will not look the other way and ignore what we do. And there is no system, or list, or set of rules, that we can follow that will ever change that fact.

So it really brings us to the place where we need to – we have to – GIVE UP…just simply GIVE UP on trying to change our behavior…GIVE UP on what's called the law. We have to GIVE UP on this idea that if we could just change…follow a certain set of rules…then God will see us differently than who we really are.

In one sense, it's a great relief, isn't it? I mean, we don't have to do that anymore. Why? Because it's useless. But in another sense, there's a lot of fear, too. "What am I going to do? What am I going to do about my character? What am I going to do about eternity? Will I be in this state forever? IF THERE'S NOTHING I CAN DO, WHAT AM I GOING TO DO?

"But now a righteousness from God…"

Today, I would like you to think about doing some journaling – some exploring. I want you to ask yourself, maybe even ask some other people, friends, co-workers, this question…If God were really righteous, what would he be like?

Have you ever heard someone say, "God's so good – I just got a great parking space." OR "God is so good – I was sick, but now I feel better." But my question is, is God good if one person found a parking space and another person didn't? Is God good if one person gets healed and another person doesn't? I mean, really! How come they got the parking space, the raise, the good buy on a great house, and I didn't? Or maybe it's me that got the great house? Is God being good to me and not to another?

Take some time and think that through as we dive into looking at God's goodness. All this week we're going to discover just how good God is. It may be too good to be true.

Apart From the Law

"But now a righteousness <u>from God</u>..."

Now, it's really important to understand this. Whose righteousness is it? Is it God's righteousness? Yes, it is. Why is it God's righteousness? It's because it's from God. It's not DIFFERENT from God's righteousness. There are not a couple of different "righteousnesses" out there. There's just one righteousness. And it's from God.

Picture this...To have righteous character means that every time you move, something good happens. Every time you have a thought, it's a good thought. Every time your hand moves, it's not only good for you, it's good for everyone else, too. Everything you say, do or think brings about good things!

Watch the sunrise one morning. Isn't it gorgeous? Isn't it beautiful? How absolutely right it seems, how cleansing and perfect! On a scale of 1 to 10, is it a 10? Well, God's righteousness is always a 10. Anything less – even a sunrise – is not like God's righteousness.

We've been discovering what God's righteousness is.

Paul says, "But now a righteousness from God apart from the law…" The law, in its most basic understanding goes back to the Ten Commandments. And the system of the law was really pretty simple. God said, "Now look…this is what I want you to do, DO IT!" In its simplest understanding it's that someone says, "I will tell you what to do. If you do what I say, you'll be blessed. If you don't do what I say, you'll be cursed." And the idea is that I will gain access to God, favor with God, based on what I DO. The law is based on what I can produce. The law is based on what I can prove. It's based on me. And so, the law may be given…it may be right…it may be good, but it's based on me, whether or not I can do it. But this   righteousness that we're going to see from God, is apart from the law. It's nothing like the law. It has   absolutely nothing to do with what I produce. It has nothing to do with God telling me what to do, and me doing it.

Ok…so, keep going…

"…this righteousness apart from the law has been made known, to which the Law and the Prophets testify." The Law and the Prophets is another way of saying "The Old Testament" The books from Genesis through Deuteronomy are called the Law, and pretty much everything after that is called the Prophets. So this is not a new idea. This righteousness was talked about in the Old Testament. It was prophesied. It is the same righteousness that we see in the Old Testament, but it has absolutely nothing to do with the law. It has nothing to do with the system of the Ten Commandments…it has nothing to do with keeping the Ten Commandments, or keeping any other system or law.

Do you remember the question from Day 2? "Is God

24

100% pleased with you?"

How did you answer the question? Was your answer a flat "NO?" Was your answer a "NO" and then you gave me a percentage based on how well you think you've been keeping the law... whatever law you think it is...whatever guidelines you've already decided... or that you've gotten from the Bible, or whatever religion you come from?

Maybe you said, "God is 50% pleased with me because I think I'm keeping 50% of the law." Well... this righteousness that we're looking at has nothing to do with that law. It's not based on what you produce. It's not based on what you're doing.

So...for your homework today, try to identify the laws that you used when you came up with that percentage...when you answered the question...Is God 100% pleased with me?

Believing in Jesus

Romans 3:21-24

So, yesterday we found out some more things about "this righteousness from God." It has nothing to do with the law, the Old Testament talks about it, and most important, it's not a second rate righteousness… it's a 10! It's 100% righteousness…from God…his righteousness.

Now…how is it passed on? How do WE get it? It "…comes through faith in Jesus Christ to all who believe." So…let's go to the end first, "…to all who believe."The simple fact is that God's righteousness is given to everyone who puts their faith in Jesus Christ…it comes through or by faith in Jesus Christ.

Well…What does it mean to have faith in Jesus Christ? Lots of people claim to believe in Jesus, all over the world. But really, believing in Jesus is actually a very personal step in a person's life. Faith is ALWAYS incredibly personal because it's about what you believe in or who you are going to trust. The word faith is actually the same word as trust. It's just that faith is the noun and trust is the verb.

Dad places his little one…his baby…standing up on the kitchen countertop, and he's laughing and giggling. And dad sticks out his arms to the baby and he says, "Now…you can jump…you can jump…come on and jump." Suppose you could interview the baby. What would the baby say? "I believe in dad…I believe he's got strong arms…I believe that he could catch me… there's no doubt about it. That's what I believe." Many times people will say, "I believe in Jesus…I believe he died for the world. I believe that he died for people's sins. I even believe he died for my sins." Well - the father says, "Jump into my arms…jump into my arms" See…It's not what the baby feels…it's not what the baby says…it's not what the baby declares…it's only when the baby jumps from the countertop into the father's arms that he has faith in the father. Faith doesn't exist in our heads. It exists in our hearts. WE ONLY KNOW IF WE HAVE IT WHEN WE DO IT.

So, when Jesus puts out his arms and he makes this promise. and he says, "Would you trust your life with the fact that I am God…that I am Jesus, the one who walked the earth 2000 years ago…that I am that man and I am actually God…I lived a perfect life…never sinned…and then I went to the cross to endure and to pay for your sin….and when I died, your sin WAS paid for…and when I rose from the dead I proved that I have power over your sin…I have power over your character. Would you put your life…your future…your eternity…into my hands? Would you jump off the countertop into my arms? If you will…if you have, then you have faith."

You stop trusting yourself…your ability to keep the law…the fact that you're a good person, trying to do a good job, having good motives. Your faith is no longer in THOSE things, but in Christ.

Here's some questions to ask yourself...

Whose arms am I in?

Who do I trust for my worth?

Who do I trust for my purpose?

Who do I trust for my eternity?

No Difference

Romans 3:22-24

Don't you hate the struggle that we have with comparing ourselves to others?

When you see others who seem to be doing this better and that better, living their lives better, maybe they worship better, earn more, make better choices. And you're just convinced… "You know what, I wish I could be like them. I wish my character was like their character. I wish I was as close to God as they are." Sometimes that way of thinking is almost crippling… we won't try new things, won't do new things, won't take risks, because we're convinced that we don't have it…we don't have what it takes.

Today we're going to check out this amazing phrase…amazing statement…as we continue in our discovery of God's righteousness. Just how good is God's righteousness? What is God's righteousness like? So…we learned yesterday that God's righteousness… this righteousness that's from God… comes though faith in Jesus Christ to all who believe. "All" is the important word here.

And Paul writes, and here's the amazing statement I just mentioned, "There is no difference..."
THERE IS NO DIFFERENCE? What's he saying?

There's no difference between those who believe in Christ because all of them are given God's goodness. And the reason there is no difference is because...here it comes... "For all have sinned and fall short of the glory of God." It's the SAME "ALL" folks!

Well, wait a minute...How much righteousness do I have in and of myself to add to the righteousness God is giving me? There's some good in everyone; right?

Go back. Remember.

God's wrath is against men who suppress the truth. God's wrath is against those who say there is no God... and ignore God. They have no righteousness of their own. God's wrath is against those who say, Well at least I don't do what they do, I'm not as bad as them... whatever rules you come up with, whatever way you come up with to judge goodness, you're going to break them, so there's no righteousness there. Even if, according to your conscience, you did as good as you possibly could...that's not true either. There's no righteousness there. There's no righteousness in the religious...the ones who claims to know the truth, and because they know the truth they MUST be good! No, because they don't keep with what they know to be true, either. It's not about what we know, it's about the heart. There is no one righteous...NOT EVEN ONE.

So how much righteousness DID we start with? ZERO. We start with nothing!

If we start with zero righteousness, every single one of us, and any righteousness that we HAVE has been given to us from God... then all we have is what HE'S GIVEN TO US.

I started with nothing...and anything I have now has nothing to do with me...it was given to me by God? CORRECT! That's right!

There is no difference because ALL of my righteousness...any goodness that's in my life...well, it came through faith. And that righteousness is perfect... It's a 10...because it comes from God. So...it doesn't matter whether I'm a pastor, a ministry leader, a small group leader, a missionary in China, an office worker, a stock broker, a janitor, a mother, a father...no matter who I am...if I place my faith in Christ...WE'RE ALL THE SAME. We have an equal amount of righteousness.

Do you know...do you understand what this does to the whole idea of a "good Christian" or a "bad Christian"...a good person or a bad person? There really aren't good people and bad people. If we have goodness, it's only a gift...a gift of GRACE.

Ah...there it is...that word GRACE.

It's something that was given to you for free...you didn't earn it. If you don't have it...well... you're a person who is just like me...YOU JUST DON'T HAVE THE GIFT.

So...I can't...can't ring my own bell or to toot my own horn...CAN'T look down on someone else. Why? Because THERE'S NO DIFFERENCE!

What freedom there is to know that we are all at the same place...all on the same level!

Justified/Redeemed

Romans 3:22-24

We're working though Romans...discovering God's righteousness. Today, as we read, we're going to notice that Paul starts writing in terms of the court system...a court of law...as if we were in a courtroom.

That said, let's go back and review.

"This righteousness from God comes through faith in Jesus Christ to all who believe. So we're talking about the "ALL"

The first thing we find out about the "all" is that there's no difference. We're ALL the same. Why? There's no difference because we "all" started with ZERO righteousness.

The second thing we find out about the "all" we can read in Romans 3:24. "...all are justified freely by his grace..."

What does it mean to be JUSTIFIED?

Well, actually, the word "justified" is the same word as "righteousness." The only difference is that "justified" is in the verb form. To be justified is to be MADE RIGHT... to be declared right. So...if we were in a court room, this is what happens to "all"…Anyone who puts their faith in Christ, God, as the judge says, "I DECLARE THIS PERSON RIGHTEOUS."

There's another word used later on…it's the word "credited" or "imputed" In other words, what happens is that God puts a righteousness from God, into your account…God says, "I declare you righteous"

So what will that cost you?

Keep reading verse 24…It says it's "…freely by his grace."

Well…Why would God do this? Why would God take those who have already been described as…<u>his wrath has been poured out because of the hurt and the pain that they've caused in other people's lives!</u> Why would he do this? I mean, it says he does it FREELY. That means I can't earn it…there's nothing I can do… nothing I can give…nothing I can pay…it's apart from the law. I can't offer God ANYTHING. He does it freely…by his grace.

GRACE! In its most simple definition, grace happens when something has been given to someone who doesn't deserve it…it's an act of giving to someone who doesn't deserve it. That's simply what it means.

So…this is the first time we actually see GRACE in our study…YES!…Finally!

Grace is the foundation of God. It's his character… it's who God is. He is gracious. And he gives away righteousness by grace. How can he do that?

"…through redemption that came by Christ Jesus."

Can God still give righteousness? Can he make me pure and good if the sin committed beforehand hasn't been paid for? The answer is no…he can't. He can't look the other way. So, what did he do? He paid for it himself. He came to earth…he became a man…he lived the life of a man, and then he said, "Now...You know what? I'm going to pay for you...for every sin you've ever committed...I'm going to put those sins on ME... and my blood pays for those sins..." The blood came through Christ Jesus. Jesus is God in human form.

Does any sin go unpunished? Nope... it doesn't. But instead of me having to pay for it, HE did!

II Corinthians 5:21 says, "God made him who had no sin to be sin for us so that in him we might become the righteousness of God." He took the sin OUT OF MY ACCOUNT and put it into JESUS' ACCOUNT! Jesus died for it...He suffered for it...He paid for it...and then he took his righteousness, and stuffed my account full! So, "If anyone is in Christ he's a new creation. The old has GONE and the NEW has come. (II Cor. 5:17)

You've been justified...and you've been redeemed. It's free...it's by grace...and it comes through faith in Jesus Christ.

Atonement

Romans 3:22-25

The next idea we're going to deal with is a word we don't use very often. It's not really a word we use in our regular language.

But first, a quick review. Ready?

We're given righteousness...righteous...freely, by his grace. How can he do that? He paid for the sin himself. He bought us...redeemed us. What did he buy us with? Christ's blood. He purchased us. He owns us. Ok...now we can go on!

"God presented him as a sacrifice of ATONEMENT..." (Romans 3:25)

That's the word that we don't use very often. ATONEMENT

"...through faith in his blood."

He just keeps saying this over and over again! It comes though faith in his blood. It's all based on a very personal decision to jump off the cliff into Jesus' arms. "Ok, Jesus. I put my future, my life, my will in your hands. You are the one that can be trusted to deal with my sins...my eternity."

Ok...so here's the question...What did God do with his anger? We're going to get to that in just a little bit.

First, here's a quick, little history lesson. In the Old Testament days they had a sacrifice of atonement... once a year. Today it is called Yom Kippur. They would sacrifice an unbelievable number of animals in order to cover over or satisfy God's wrath because there is no forgiveness without the shedding of blood. (Heb 9:22) God would accept that blood from those animals to cover over their sin. And it would satisfy his wrath. That was atonement in the Old Testament times. But what does atonement look like today?

Well, the word ATONEMENT really works like this...

If you're a car lover you're really going to relate to this. If not...well...you'll be able to relate to it with something else you value and love.

Ok...so you've been saving your money for ions... saving and saving and saving...and FINALLY you have enough for your dream car...whatever your dream car might be. It cost $50,000! And you didn't even take a loan out on the car...you paid cash. YOU BOUGHT THE CAR! Of course, it took every cent of what you saved, so you only took out PLPD insurance... uh...that's Personal Liability/Personal Damages for those of us who need to know. That means that in case there's an accident, the insurance won't pay to fix your car, just theirs.

Now...you're out driving along...really savoring the moment, when some smart alleck passes you, laughing at you, making fun of you and how slow you're driving. They're fooling around and kind of slinging in front of you and in back of you...mocking you. HOW ANNOYING! So you don't see him for a few miles, and

36

then you come to a stop light. It's green, you go through it, and just as you're getting through the intersection another person comes through the stop light…they run the red light and they smash into the side of your car…and your car is totaled…they just DESTROY your car!

You're ok. But you get out of your car, and that's when you realize that the guy that just demolished your beautiful dream car is actually the same person who was mocking you earlier! You are FURIOUS…you should be furious. That person has done you wrong. He has truly sinned against you. And you're walking around fuming and just thinking, "This person has to pay BIG TIME!" You have WRATH for that person.

So then, the person gets out of the car, looks over the situation, walks over to you…and YOU ARE READY TO GIVE HIM A PIECE OF YOUR MIND! And before you can really let loose on him, he says, "Wow. This was totally my fault. I'll tell you what…here's $200,000 cash. Will this take care of it? I really want to make up for this." And your mouth drops open….you can't believe it! AS SOON AS HE PUTS THAT CASH INTO YOUR HAND…YOUR ANGER IS GONE. You go from, "This guy is a total jerk!" to "Hey, I kind of like this guy."

Well…that's ATONEMENT. He just atoned for what he did. He paid for it. He made up for it.

God presented Jesus as a SACRIFICE OF ATONEMENT.

The Bible says that, "it pleased God to bruise him…" (Isaiah 53:10)

Sometimes we think, well, Satan is the one who put Jesus on the cross…Satan was the one that beat him. That's not true. Jesus chose to go to the cross. What happened was that God the father bruised God the son...he poured out his wrath on Christ. On the cross Jesus was paying the price for all the damage we have done toward God and others.

Think about all of the wrath that God would have about the sins we've committed. We're not even thinking about all the sins. We're just thinking about the wrath. Think about how angry God is for the lies, the attitude, the mean things we've said, the countless ways we've hurt people. And we're not even going to the things that he's angry about in terms of the good things he would have had us done, but we were too busy being selfish...too busy thinking of ourselves... living for ourselves. Just think about the wrath that God would have at all of that and then put it all into a container. For me, it would be a huge trainload of containers. In fact, I can't think of anything that would be THAT big that would be able to hold all the wrath that God has for me.

God took all that wrath...for my sin, every sin I've ever committed...all the sin I ever will commit, and he poured that out on Christ. He turned my container up side down on Christ. When Jesus was on the cross he said, "My God, My God, How could you have forsaken me?" All that loneliness...all that separation...all that anger that Jesus had to endure for every sin I've ever committed was in that container!

Now...take that container, and turn it right back up.

What kind of a relationship do I have with God? If I trusted in Christ...this has happened to me...for me... what kind of a relationship do I have with God?

"Oh, God's disappointed because I did that, and I did this." and "Oh, he's disgusted because I did that." and "He's got to be angry about this..." We do that act, but the bottom line is that when I climb to the top of the rim of that container, and look down at God's anger….that container is empty. God is NOT angry. Why? It's because the anger is gone. It's already been poured out. God will never, ever be disgusted or angry with me again.

I think that's way too good to be true.

Living by Grace: You will have plenty of people who get mad at you or will be disappointed with you. Eyes will roll, the shoulders slump, the voice will rise. Most of the time it will be you toward yourself. When you notice, trade in their opinion for your God's opinion. Trade in what you're thinking for what God thinks and watch the peace flow.

God Is So Good
He Makes Others Good As Well

Romans 3:25-26

Have you ever met someone who is good? Do you know some good people?

Sometimes we come across people who are "the best"...and when we see the best, you know what that does? It kind of acts like a mirror and points out to us that we're not the best. What does THE BEST look like?

Maybe they're the leader of a company. They're so focused on being the best that they use everyone around them just so that they can be the best. And in their wake they leave a group of people who know they've seen the best, but once they are gone, they are gone, because it really was all about them.

Then there's the leader that demands the best...he is the best...and he motivates others to be their best, do their best. This leader can produce an organization of people who maybe aren't necessarily the best, but because they work together, and because he has such a high standard, he motivates them toward that standard. So, maybe the organization is not perfect, but it's still a really good organization because he used everyone there. He helped them to take the next step and move up.

Sometimes we see God like that, where God is concerned about our behavior, what we do, how we perform. He wants our behavior to change so that good things can happen.

But then there's a particular leader whom we've never seen…never been exposed to. In fact, we really have no model to understand this type of leader. This leader not only IS the best, but everyone around him can SEE that he is the best. He is the standard that we all want and should aspire to. When this leader goes to work each day, he touches others. He pays the price for them to become good like he is. As he moves and walks, he touches people, and what he leaves in his wake, are people, an entire family, an entire company, who has the same goodness that he has.

That's what we've learned that God is REALLY like. God takes people who were wicked and evil and selfish, and he turns them into loving, righteous, pure people. In other words…he takes his character, and he puts it inside of them.

Pretty cool, huh?

Why would he do that? Well, go back to verse 25. It says that he did it to "demonstrate his justice…" (his goodness) "…because in his forbearance he had left the sins committed before him unpunished." You see, for all of the sins that were committed BEFORE Jesus died on the cross to pay for them, God was patient. He was so good that he had forbearance…he put up with them. That's what the Old Testament sacrifice was for… the blood of the sacrifice COVERED those sins until that day…the day Jesus paid for them…it didn't pay for them. And God "patiently waited with" those sins because he knew that day was coming. "He did it to demonstrate his justice at the present time…" that's for US…that's for you and me. "…so as to be just…" God is not only righteous, he's the one who justifies those who have faith in Jesus. Put simply…he's not only good, he makes everyone he touches good too!

Ok. Here's what it comes down to…it comes down to a choice…he leaves you with a choice.

Will you jump off the cliff into Jesus' arms? Will you trust the goodness of God? Will you give up trying? Will you give up control of your life? Will you put your eternity, your marriage, your dreams, your wants… will you put EVERYTHING into his hands? Whatever you have YOU CAN'T MAKE IT GOOD. So would you give up trying and jump into Jesus' arms and let him make you pure? Let him pay for your sin? Let him sacrifice? Let him atone for…make up for all the hurt that you've caused in life, and all the hurt you're going to cause in your life?

Faith vs. Law

Romans 4:1-4

"If God wrote the Bible, and the Bible teaches the same thing, then why are there so many different religions in the world? If there is a God, why can't we just agree about who he is and what he's like?

Well, actually, the Bible teaches that there really aren't a whole bunch of different kinds of religions in the world. There are just two...Faith or Law.

Faith is when I come to God based on what he's done. God has promised me something...he offers me something...and I put my faith in what he says and what he offers.

Law is different. Law is the system where God says, "Ok...Here's your list." Maybe the list is the Ten Commandments. And God says. "Keep that list...obey that list." And if I can keep the list, then I'm good   before God...he's happy with me...pleased with me. But if I break the list, then he's no longer happy with me, and I have to rebuild my relationship with him...really focus on what I can do to make God pleased with me.

So, Paul has introduced us to an incredible truth.

God, through Jesus Christ, is offering us a brand new life where he offers to pay for our sin. He offers to satisfy God's wrath so that God will never be angry at us again. He offers this whole brand new relationship entirely based on faith…entirely based on God making a promise to us, and then we live our lives based on THE PROMISE. That's what we follow. That's what we trust. That's where we put our hearts.

Now for someone who is Jewish – or anyone who reads the Bible – there's a question about THE PROMISE.

"Hey, wait a minute! Is this really brand new? What about Abraham? Abraham was the father of many nations. Abraham was the one who got the promise in the first place, right?

And Paul, always on his toes, says, "What then shall we say that Abraham, our forefather, discovered in this matter? If in fact, Abraham was justified by works, he has something to boast about – but not before God." See…if Abraham lived such a good life, kept the law in such a way that he could say, "Ok…my just wages is that I am righteous. My just wages is that I am just" then he could boast about what HE did to become righteous. But interesting enough, Paul says, NOT BEFORE GOD.

What does it say in chapter 4?

"Abraham BELIEVED GOD and it was credited to him as righteousness."

So the same principle applies to the Old Testament as it does to the New Testament. The WORDS of the promise were different. And the promise hadn't come yet…Christ hadn't come yet to forgive our sins so that if we trust in him we can be forgiven. But Abraham was given the promise that it WAS COMING…the

Messiah was coming one day.

"Now when a man works, his wages are not credited to him as a gift, but as an obligation."

Labor is really a very simple system. When I go to work for someone, at the end of the day, when I get my wages, the employer is not doing me a favor. He's not giving me grace by paying me. It was a deal I worked out with the employer. We're on equal ground...I made a contract...kind of like a covenant. The employer will pay so much per hour...say he pays $8 per hour, and at the end of the day, if I worked 8 hours, I should get $64. I deserve the $64 dollars because it's based on the work that I did. It's based on what I produced.

Well, that's the relationship of the law. But NOW look at this!

"However, to the man who does NOT work but trusts God who justifies the wicked, his faith is credited as righteousness."

It's the person who DOESN"T work. It's the person who has a relationship with someone who says, "I want to give you a gift. I want to impact your life. Out of my goodness...out of my grace... I want to give you a gift of $64." The only action that you can take is to TRUST him.

That's the relationship of FAITH. How does that work?

Well, ok....you don't work all day. At the end of the day, the question is, "Will the employer... the man who made the promise...KEEP HIS PROMISE? If he does, then I can trust him...if he does, I'll trust him ALL DAY! I'll live the whole day as if at the end of the day I will be given that $64. And at the end of the day...I GET IT! Now that's a totally different system.

The two systems cannot mix in any way, shape or form. You can't work for an hour and then trust him for the rest of it. You can't work for 15 minutes and then trust him for the rest of it. If you work even one minute, then you've entered into the system of the law. Then you have a different relationship with the employer or the person who has the gift to give. That relationship is the relationship of the law. If you have faith, it's in his PROMISE and in his promise ALONE. It's not in what YOU can do. If you live under the law, then your faith is in what you can produce.

Let's go back to Abraham. Paul says that Abraham had a relationship with God that was by faith. It's the same new relationship that God wants us to have with him...it's through Jesus Christ, by faith.

And Paul says that David had that kind of relationship with God, too. So as he writes, he includes this little excerpt from something that David wrote.

"...the blessedness of the man to whom God credits righteousness apart from works. Blessed are they whose transgressions are forgiven, whose sins are covered. Blessed is the man whose sin the Lord will never count against him."

It means that David didn't mix the law and faith, either. He trusted God for WHAT GOD HAD PROMISED HIM! He was forgiven because of what God promised him, not because of the way he had lived.

Go back to the very first question I asked you when we began this journey...Is God 100% pleased with you? Look that up. What was the number you gave?

If you said, "No, God isn't 100% pleased with me" and then you gave a percentage, whatever percentage you gave, that's the percentage you live by the law... how well you think you're doing.

46

So…if you gave yourself 10 %, then you believe…
"I'm 10% good. I've worked and I deserve 10%…10% of my life deserves to be pleased by God." If you gave yourself 50%, then you're saying that 50% of your life deserves to be pleased by God. If you gave 75%…90%… really what you're saying is, "I have the kind of relationship with God that when I live the way he wants me to live then he's pleased with me, and when I don't, he's not."

BUT…Everything we've learned up to this point is… GOD DOES NOT RELATE TO US THAT WAY!

We're either righteous or we're not righteous. We're either going to trust that at the end of the day God will keep his promise…he will make us just…he will forgive us…He will put his righteousness in our character…or we believe we have to earn it.

Which one is it for you? In what areas of your life have you been trying to live by the law? In what areas would you say, "No…I can trust God."?

How Do I Believe?

Romans 4:16-20

If it comes down to law and faith, and the Bible teaches that we come to know God's grace by faith… we can actually see his righteousness by faith, then it's pretty important that we understand what faith is.

People throw the word "faith" around a lot.

When someone goes through a great tragedy, people ask, "How did you get through it?" And many times they answer, "I got through it by my faith." Or sometimes, people will say, "He's a man of deep faith….or deep convictions." But faith is really SO SIMPLE that it almost seems hard to grab hold of.

Faith is either ALL or NOTHING. You either trust in something all the way or you don't trust in it at all. What if I trust in it 99%? Nope! If you leave off that 1% then you're not really trusting…you still think you need to do something to be able to make it happen.

Faith is perfectly illustrated in Romans 4:18-21 where Paul continues writing about Abraham's faith in God.

To really understand this we need a little bit of background in the life of Abraham. He had been given a promise by God. Part of that promise was that he

48

would be the father of many nations... he'd have lots and lots of children. Back then a man really measured himself based on what he left behind, so it was really important to him that he have children, who would have children, who would have children, and so on... and in this way his name would always be known because he had built a great nation.

So God had made him this promise...it was going to happen to HIM. But he lived a good many years...100 years, in fact, and he still hadn't had a child. After 100 years you've got to be thinking, "THIS IS NOT GOING TO HAPPEN" Then God comes to him again, and he repeats this promise. And I'm thinking, "It doesn't matter how many times you repeat that promise...I'm 100 years old!" Well...Abraham was thinking the same thing!! "Yeah...right...do you realize that I'm now 100 years old and it's going to be impossible for me to have kids?"

God is patient. He just smiles and says, "Come on outside for a moment...I want you look up at the stars." Look up at the STARS! And Abraham does it... he looks up at the sky...and it's filled with stars. And then God says to him ever so gently, "As many stars as you see...that's how many children you're going to have." No...he doesn't mean that Abraham will literally have all those children. He means that any children, of children, of children, would be considered his children.

And what Romans says, it's in verse 18, about that event is, "Against all hope, Abraham in hope BELIEVED and so became the father of many nations, JUST AS IT HAD BEEN SAID TO HIM...Without weakening in his faith, he faced the fact that his body was as good as dead."

Did you catch it? Even though he faced the fact that his body was as good as dead, he didn't weaken in his faith!

There are two parts to faith.

The first part is that you must TAKE A GOOD LOOK AT REALITY. Faith that is grounded in "pie in the sky" or in the idea that we can't really understand God, is not faith. God doesn't want us to live only in the spiritual world. He wants us to see the real world. To have true faith you have to take a look at what the circumstances really are...what's the reality of the circumstances.

Abraham looked at his body and said, "It's as good as dead...I'm 100 years old...I'm at the end of my life... I have been trying to have a child for at least 70 years...my body doesn't work." His wife's body didn't work, either. Sarah's womb was also dead. He looked at the facts, and according to what he understood the facts to be, it just wasn't possible. But look at verse 20. "Yet, he did not waver through unbelief regarding the promise of God."

The second part of faith is IDENTIFYING THE PROMISE OF GOD. Faith doesn't work if you come up with something that's not what God promised. "I trusted God that I would have a great job...I trusted God that I would do well in my career...I trusted God we'd win the game..." Well...none of those are   promises from God. You can't place your faith in God if he didn't make a promise to you.

Abraham took a look at the reality of his circumstances...it was impossible for him to have children with Sarah...and then he identified God's promise. God did make him a specific promise, and he made a choice...it's the rest of verse 20. "But with

50

strength in his faith he gave glory to God, being fully persuaded that God had the power to do what he had promised."

And THAT is why it was credited to him as righteousness. He looked at his circumstances...he looked at God's promise...who God was...and he chose to trust, to put his life, to put his heart in what God said. At that very moment, God put righteousness in his account. It was at that moment that Abraham became a believer.

You know what? It's true! I can know that what I trust will happen IS GOING TO HAPPEN. Why? God promised it to me.

It's as simple as I said it was, right? Now really read this next part. It's WAY important. Read it again and again if you need to...

God has made you a promise. He has promised you forgiveness, righteousness. He's promised that his wrath will be taken away...it will be satisfied. HE'S PROMISED THAT TO YOU!

Because of the power of Jesus Christ...the power of his death on the cross...and his resurrection, he has promised you a brand new life.

If you're looking at your circumstances, and thinking...this is impossible. It's impossible that I could ever become a righteous, pure person, because I know who I am. The question is...

Am I going to trust those circumstances or am I going to trust God's promise...what God says is true? Write out a prayer to God sharing with him the promises you trust him to keep.

Grace Guarantees Promise

Romans 4:16

The strength of a guarantee is based on the person who makes the guarantee.

If you buy something off the TV, they usually say, "This is guaranteed...it got a lifetime warranty." You get the warranty...it's a beautiful certificate promising a great warranty...lifetime guarantee. If it ever breaks, if anything ever goes wrong with it, just send it back to them and they will send back every cent of the money you paid for it...minus shipping charges, of course.

You know that guarantee is only good if the person who wrote it is faithful. It's only good if they have the power to enforce it. It's only good if they have a character to keep their word.

Why does THE PROMISE only come by faith? Today we're going to see that the reason is so that it can be GUARANTEED.

If you own a vehicle you know that to maintain it well you have to have good tires. If you've bought new tires, you know that they usually carry a warranty... something like, 60,000 miles as long as you rotate the tires every 15,000 miles. So we drive, and drive, and drive, not paying a whole lot of attention to that "15,000 mile thing" and then one day you notice that they're starting to wear out, and you definitely haven't driven 60.000 miles! You take the car back and they say, "MMMM…looks to me like you didn't rotate these the way you were suppose to."

That guarantee is no good because that guarantee is not just based on the person who gave it. It was based on the person it was given to…the one who didn't rotate the tires. A little bit of the law gets mixed in… you've got to do something for the guarantee to be valuable…to be worth anything.

Look at Romans 4:16

"Therefore, the promise…"

What is THE PROMISE? The promise is forgiveness, it's righteousness, it's a perfect relationship with God… the kind of relationship where he is always pleased with me.

"…comes by faith…"

I look at the facts…the circumstances. Based on the way I'm living there's no way God's going to be pleased with me. And I look at what God says… "You know what? I'll pay for it. I'll pay for everything you've done wrong. I'm offering you a brand new life that I will pay for totally by myself…by grace…a gift you don't deserve…it has nothing to do with your value…nothing to do with what you produce.

"… so that it may be grace and may be guaranteed to all Abraham's offspring…"

The only way that the promise can be guaranteed is if it only and totally depends on God to keep his promise. See…God never lies. He has the power to bring righteousness and life into people's lives. HE

HAS MORE GOODNESS TO GIVE AWAY THAN HE KNOWS WHAT TO DO WITH! Only he can guarantee THE PROMISE. And all we can do is accept it. We either reject it or accept it. We don't earn it...it's given to us even though we don't deserve it. We can't deserve it. If we deserve it it's not by grace...and therefore it's not guarantee.

"...not only to those who are of the law but also those who are of the faith of Abraham. He is the father of us all."

Every person from the beginning of creation to this very day and forward...every person who has placed their faith in the promise of God...WE'RE ALL IN THE SAME FAMILY! We have all received from God his righteousness and goodness. We have all gone through the same door..."God... I have nothing to offer you... nothing at all. But you made me a promise, and I accept that promise."

So what are you trusting to guarantee God's pleasure? What are you trusting to guarantee God's blessing in your life? What are you trusting for success in your relationships? What are you trusting to make your life work? Is it the promise of God or is it something else?

How Do I Stand In Grace?

Romans 5:1-3

PEACE.

We're all seeking peace…we all so badly want peace. No more war inside of our hearts. No more war inside of our souls. We want peace among men. We want peace in our families. We hate to walk into a place that is filled with conflict. We even pray for peace… "God give me peace…" The Bible talks about peace…how God wants to give us peace in our hearts…

"Therefore, since we have been justified through faith, we have peace with God through our Lord Jesus Christ…" (5:1)

Today you're getting a chance to practice your faith. Take a look at your life, take a look at the consequences of your circumstances, take a look at the circumstances as you see them. Doesn't it scream at you…doesn't everything inside of you tell you…"You know what… there's no peace between God and I…God must be so disappointed with me. He must be so disgusted…he must be so angry." Maybe it's vice versa…maybe it's the opposite. Maybe it's that you are frustrated with God…you're mad at God…you feel like… "You know what?…God and I are not on the same side."

The definition of peace is this…NO CONFLICT. There's no longer any conflict.

But it's stronger than that. It's not just that there's no conflict. It's that we're on the same side. We are headed in the same direction. We are in step with one another. We are at peace with each other.

"Therefore, since we have been justified…" Therefore since God has made us right…Therefore since he has made us pure and holy in his sight…

"…through faith we have peace with God."

Your circumstances may scream at you that there is no peace…you need peace, but God promises…HE SAYS IT'S A FACT…"I'm at peace with you." Why? "I'm at peace with you because I've made myself at peace with you."

We don't have peace with God because we kept the law…it's not about how well we live. We don't have peace with God because we did our quiet time or because we were nice to people or because we were honest at work. We don't have peace with God because we've guaranteed it ourselves…we've done something to make the warranty stand up. We have peace with God because he made us a promise. What was the promise again? "I'll take your place…I'll pay for everything you've ever done wrong to me."

We really do have peace, because God has made peace with us!

So…where are you going to put your faith? Is your faith in the way you feel? Is your faith in what you think? Is your faith in what you see? Or is your faith in what God has promised?

"Through whom…" and he's talking about Jesus here, "…we have gained access by faith into this grace in which we now stand."

Grace is the place where you stand. It's who you have   become. It's where you live your life. As far as God is concerned, from the time that you placed your faith in the blood of Jesus Christ…from that day forward… YOU STAND IN GRACE. You're not measured by what you produce, what you do, what you think. You stand in a place of peace, not because you deserve it, but by grace. You stand in a place of peace because God has kept his promise to you. How do you gain access to that place? You gain access by faith…by looking at your circumstances as they are…looking at what God has promised you, and putting your faith in God and his power to keep the promise he's given to you.

Try this today: Three times today close your eyes, close out as much noise as possible and thank God for the new relationship of peace that he has with you. Ask yourself, "Is God at peace with me? Why am I angry? What else do I need?" When you're finished, e-mail me some other ways that knowing God gives you a "peace" that has changed your life:

Chris@skylinenj.org

Grace vs. Law

Romans 5:12-19

Today we're going to review a principle that's going to be really important as we work through our journey of grace.

We are not separated from God simply because of what we do, but because of who we are.
Do you ever picture God kind of like a judge sitting on his throne...looking at what we've done and saying, "Ok, now wait a minute...we've got the scales tipping back and forth...he did this amount good, but he did this amount bad, and so...ooooh...ooooh...Rats!...He's a bad egg."

Many times it's our parents that interacted with us this way...bosses interact with us this way, our neighbors interact with us this way, our friends...We're always being judged based on what we do and what we produce.

But it's not just because of what we do that we are separated from God, that we die, it's because of who we are. That's what Paul writes about in Romans 5:12. "Therefore, just as sin entered the world through one man, and death through sin, and in this way death came to all men, because all sinned..."

One man...Death...all sinned? What are you saying? He's saying we are actually born into sin...we are born sinners. Adam sinned, we were part of him...we come from him...he was separated from God... and that passed on to us. His sin created death in our lives. Keep going...you will get this soon!

"...for before the law was given sin was in the world. But sin is not taken into account when there is no law. Nevertheless death reigned from the time of Adam to the time of Moses..."

I know this will sound a bit confusing at first...but bear with me.

His point is that we are all dead under sin. He proves it because people died even though their slates were clean. This amazed me when I found it...when I realized what he was saying. But the truth is that when there is no law, when God has not given specific commands to you, he does not write it down when you do it. So if God hasn't told you not to lie, when you lie, he does not write it down. There is no "Accounting Ledger" with good stuff on one side and sins or transgressions on the other side. The law was given by Moses, so for the people who lived from the time of Adam up to the time Moses gave the law, their accounts were clean. And yet they died. Why? Because of who they were, not because of what they had done...because they were sin.

The same is true for God's wrath against us. God is not simply mad because of what we do. Sometimes people mock and say, "oooooooh, what is God going to do, send me to hell because I stole a piece of paper or smoked some weed or looked at a little porno?"

59

Actually, no, he isn't. He isn't going to send you to hell over those things. He is going to send you to hell because of who you are.

We have to understand that in our relationship with God, it is not just what we've done that God judges us...it's who we are that he judges us. He relates to us based on who we are, not just what we've done. That's how the system of the law works.

So, that kind of leaves us with a question.

Who am I?

How Do I Get More Grace?

Romans 5:20-21

This is my favorite part of Romans. I enjoy watching my own reaction, still, and I'm going to enjoy watching your reaction, as well.

It's in Romans 5:15-21…

Yesterday Paul declared that we are judged not just on what we do, but who we are, and we were left with a question… "Well then…Who am I?

And he said that we can really be from 1 of 2 people. We can either be from Adam, or we can be from Jesus. Very simply, Adam's one act causes certain things to happen, and Jesus' one act causes, really, the opposite things to happen.

So what happened after Adam's one act?

When Adam sinned against God, when he knew exactly what God had to say, and he said "No…I don't trust you…I trust myself…I'm going to do it my way"…and he rebelled against God…this is what happened: Many died, judgment took place, many were condemned, death reigned in all, and many were made sinners. Romans 5:15-19

The opposite happened when Jesus died on the cross for us...his one act. And when we place our faith in him, this is what happens: God's grace overflows to many, there's justification, righteousness reigns in lives, and many were made good. Romans 5:15-19

Look at who you are...which one of these do you follow? Are you from Adam? Is your faith in yourself, or some other way of getting to God...some way of earning your place before him? Or are you from Jesus, the one in whom your entire faith...all of your trust...is in his promise and his ability to keep that promise?

He makes this amazing statement..."The law was added so the trespass might increase."

Do you remember that Accounting Ledger we talked about where on the one side I did good, on the other side I did bad? The bad side...it was completely clean...it was pure, because it's not written down since there is no law. Then the law came, and it began to be written down. And what happened was, the sin side, the trespass side began to fill up in amazing ways...it began to fill up with just mark after mark after mark.

Well...What's so amazing about that?

It says, "But where sin increased..." THIS IS WHERE IT STARTS TO GET AMAZING!

Look at your life...I'm looking at mine. If I take every word, every thought, every attitude, every action that I do that is selfish, that is not righteous, it's not pure, it's not good, it's not for others, it's not according to what God has to say. It's just my own thing, whatever my own thing is... well...in a period of a day, you're going to have, what, 100, 500, 1000 things, if we include our thoughts, that are GOING TO BE ON THE TRESSPASS SIDE OF THE LEDGER.

NOW HERE IT IS...ARE YOU READY FOR THE BEST

PART?

"...where sin increased, GRACE INCREASED ALL THE MORE..." That's it! That's the best part!

The more I have written on the wrong side, the more grace God gives to me. That's the exact definition of grace.

You see...the only way that I can get grace is...I can't deserve it. The only way I can get God's blessing by grace is when I don't deserve it. The only way I can get God's forgiveness by grace is when I don't deserve it. And so...how would I get more of God's grace. If this is true...how do I get more of God's grace? What's the answer? By sinning!!!

"...so that just as sin reigned in death, so also grace might reign through righteousness to bring eternal life through Jesus Christ our Lord."

Ok...so try this little experiment.

Try to get as much grace as you can possibly get between now and tomorrow.

I mean, here's the thing. Jesus died on the cross, he's paid for every sin that you will ever commit, so when you sin, what you get is LOTS OF GOD'S GRACE, right? That means God's going to pay attention to you, he's going to spend time with you, he's going to be interested in you, he's going to pour out his goodness, his grace...into your life...if you sin.

Knowing that's true...knowing that he loved you so much that he would die for you, why not pick a sin or two...one that you struggle with, and say, "You know what?...I'm going to do this because I know that God will not condemn me. He will not be angry with me. He will only forgive me. He'll just pour grace into my life if I do this...and see what happens.

Why Do I Still Sin?

Romans 5:20-21

Well…How'd your day go?

Did you test it out?

Would you do something for me? Would you just write down what happened as you tried to get as much grace as possible? Just jot it down right here in your devotional book. Tell me just how that went…what you learned…what you experienced…and then, if you would, email that to me, Pastor Chris, or to your Life Group Leader. Thanks!

This is a good halfway point. We'd like to know how things are going, and what you're learning…what you're experiencing as you seek to be free, as you discover God's grace.

The Sin

Romans 7:7-12

Ok...we're going to jump ahead a little bit...we're going to head over to Romans 7:7-12.

Two sins...that's what we're talking about, and as we do it's going to be something that's really helpful to you as you move forward through chapters 6 and 7.

Paul talks about two kinds of sin, or better put, he talks about two different ways we sin. The first is "THE SIN" ...that's what happened to us...that's who we became when Adam ate the fruit after God told him not to. We've all experienced it...it's very simple, really. Whenever someone tells us not to do something... we want to do it.

Let's try it out.

Right now...if I say, "Ok, now don't look at the light. Whatever you do, don't look at the light...if you look at the light bad things are going to happen, or if you don't look at the light, good things will happen...DON'T LOOK AT THE LIGHT!" There's something inside of us that WANTS TO LOOK AT THE LIGHT. It's just like that "drawing the line in the sand." When someone draws a line in the sand and says, "Don't jump over that line"…there's just something inside of us that wants to jump over that line. That's called "the sin"… it's this rebellion. It's…"I will do what I want to do, and no one else is going to tell me what to do!" We're all born with it. We all have it.

In the Greek language you can tell the difference between the two, but in the English you can't. In the Greek they put an article in front of it…and it always follows that article. For those of us who are not Grammar buffs, the article is just kind of like the word "the" so this one with the article is what happened to us as a result of Adams one act.

The second sin has no article…it's sin that's trans- gression. It's an act of sin. It's when we actually sin, curse, lie, or steal. When we actually do the act of sin- ning, it's called a transgression. The first one is who we are…the second one is what we do.

So…How does THE SIN work? How does it work out as it relates to our lives?

"What shall we say, then? Is the law THE SIN? Certainly not! Indeed I would not have known what THE SIN was except through the law. For I would not have known what coveting really was if the law had not said, 'Do not covet' But THE SIN, seizing the opportunity afforded by the commandment, produced in me every kind of covetous desire. For apart from the law, THE SIN is dead"

That's a really important principle. It's going to come into play as we work our way though Romans 6&7, as we begin to understand grace, and as we realize what it means to live outside of the box. And most of us DO believe that God DOES have a box. He has a set of rules…commands…expectations for us, and if we live inside of that box, then we're safe. But what this is teaching us is that if there is no box, then the law is dead.

"Once I was alive apart from the law, but when the commandment came, THE SIN SPRANG TO LIFE and I died.

Oh, yeah! That's how it works, alright!

As soon as God told me what to do or what not to do, as soon as that happened, then THE SIN came to life in me and I said, "Ok...I'm gonna do it!" Verse 10 says, "I found that the very commandment that was intended to bring life actually brought death." So when God says don't lie, don't commit adultery, both of those things are going bring life into you...God says, "I command you to live like this". Somehow...THE SIN just comes to life!

"For the sin, seizing the opportunity afforded by the commandment, deceived me, and through the commandment put me to death. So then, the law is holy..."

The 10 commandments, the Bible, the Old Testament... They say good things...

"...and the commandment is holy, and righteous and good. Did that which is good, then, become death to me? By no means! But in order that the sin might be recognized as sin, it produced death in me through what was good, so that through the commandment "The sin" might become utterly sinful."

Put simply, through the commandment, because of the commandment, we saw just how sinful we were.

Just picture that box and the person inside it...or picture that line that you drew in the sand. Are you hearing that voice that says, "Now if you do this, I won't be pleased with you...don't do that!"

That's the way THE SIN works. THE SIN rules our lives. It reigns in our lives. We are a slave to it. That's who we are.

Where you see the word sin underlined it is where the article appears in Greek referring to the sin Adam passed onto us, our sin nature.

*What shall we say, then? Is the law sin? Certainly not! Indeed I would not have known what **sin** was except through the law. For I would not have known what coveting really was if the law had not said, "Do not covet." But **sin**, seizing the opportunity afforded by the commandment, produced in me every kind of covetous desire. For apart from law, **sin** is dead. Once I was alive apart from law; but when the commandment came, **sin** sprang to life and I died. I found that the very commandment that was intended to bring life actually brought death.*

*For **sin**, seizing the opportunity afforded by the commandment, deceived me, and through the commandment put me to death. So then, the law is holy, and the commandment is holy, righteous and good. Did that which is good, then, become death to me? By no means! But in order that **sin** might be recognized as sin, it produced death in me through what was good, so that through the commandment **sin** might become utterly sinful.* Romans 7:7-13

Why Not Sin?

Romans 6:1-7

If you've understood what we've been reading the last couple of days, then you've been practicing sinning because you've been practicing gaining grace, right?

How do you do that? You do it by sinning more. So then the obvious question is...well...Why not sin? I mean, if we get more grace by sinning, then, why not keep sinning?

Congratulations!

That's exactly the question Paul asked, as well. And that's great because then we know that we've truly understood what the previous passage was teaching because Paul comes up with the exact same question. He expects us to ask that question.

It seems there are as many ways to answer that question as there are religions or churches. Everyone seems to have a different list to tell us why we shouldn't sin, and even what sin is.

But I'm curious what you have to say. Why would you not sin? Maybe you'd say it's because God doesn't like it, or that God will get angry at you. Maybe you're thinking you wouldn't because you'll have to pay for it in some form or fashion…like…what goes around, comes around?

Just take a few minutes, right now, and jot down all the reasons that you, personally, practice not to sin. How do you try to stop sinning? Why is it that you do that? Maybe a better question is how do you try to change your life…and why do you do that? What is it that you're trying to do to make yourself different than who you know yourself to be right now?

Great! Now let's review.

We've been asking the same question for a couple of days now…Who are you? God doesn't judge you just based on what you do, but who you are. And we found out that the more you do wrong, the more grace you get. So that's what lead us to the question…Why not sin?

Now…Paul gives the most amazing answer to this question…and it's quite simple, really. The answer is because that's NOT who you are…

"What shall we say, then? Shall we go on sinning so that grace may increase? BY NO MEANS! We died to sin; how can we live in it any longer?"

Remember when we talked about Adam, and who you are…Are you of Adam? Are you of Jesus? He says if you've trusted Christ…if your faith is in Christ, then you are of Christ, and you've been baptized. What THAT means is, you've been   immersed… dunked in…put into…YOU ARE IN CHRIST…that's who you are. You belong to Jesus Christ.

Check out verse 6… "…therefore buried with him through baptism into death in order that just as Christ was raised from the dead through the glory of the Father, we too may live a new life."

In other words, YOU'RE A NEW PERSON!

70

Who am I?

The answer to the question is…I'm with Christ… that' who I am…I belong to him.

Say it again, out loud! If you've trusted Jesus…your faith is in him…WHO ARE YOU?

I'M WITH CHRIST…I BELONG TO HIM.

"For we know that our old self was crucified with him so that the body of sin might be done away with…"

The person we were born to be, the person who was born dead…the person who was born in Adam…that person died on the cross. That person no longer lives.

"…because anyone who has died has been freed from sin."

The simple answer to "Why not sin?" is…THAT'S NOT WHO I AM…THAT'S NOT WHO I SERVE.

You've got to practice faith here. Don't depend on your feelings, because your feelings, and lots of times your desires tell you the EXACT OPPOSITE of what the truth is. But God says, this is who you are. Who are you going to trust? Who are you going to put your faith in? When you answer the question, "Who am I" are you going to answer it according to the way you feel? Or…Are you going to take a look at the circumstances, then take a look at what God promises, and choose what God promises?

Alive unto God

Romans 6:8-11

Have you ever eaten something really delicious, and then said, "Wow, that's SO good. That's just too good to be true!" And then someone says to you, "Yea, but now try this...gets even better..." Well that's what happens today as we take a look at who we are, and what it means to stand in grace.

Yesterday we covered that we're dead to sin...that that's not who we are anymore...and we live with Christ. See THAT in verse 8, "Now if we die with Christ, we believe that we will also live with him..."

Ok...that's NOT who I am, I live with Christ, but...

"For we know that since Christ was raised from the dead, he cannot die again; death no longer has mastery over him."

He won! He already experienced death, and he won. He did it, conquered it....WON!

When you took your very, very first step as a young child, you were afraid. You know that if you've ever helped a child take that first step. They're afraid to take that step. But once they take that step, then you know what? They can never go back to NOT WALKING again. Why? The child has experienced the delight of walking and has mastered it.

That's what Christ did. He will never, ever die again, because all of the sin, all of the death of the world was poured out on him, and yet HE STILL WON! He was victorious! He was more powerful than death.

"The death he dies, he died to sin once for all; but the life he lives, he lives to God."

Now, think about that…

Ok…so he died to sin, so that's gone and finished. But the life he lives he lives to God. How much do you think Jesus lives to God? How much do you think he wants to do exactly what God the Father wants? How much do you think God the Son wants to do what God the Father wants? Do you think maybe 10% of the time? How about 50% of the time? Well you say, "You're being foolish." Every breath, every thought, everything about who Jesus is…he wants to do exactly what God wants. That's what he wants. There's no conflict…there's no war between what God the Son wants and what God the Father wants.

Well, here's the amazing part, and again, this is going to take faith.

Paul says, "In the same way, count yourselves dead to sin but alive to God in Christ Jesus."
YOU want to do what God wants… just like Jesus does. That's going to take faith, isn't it? Because when you look at your circumstances, and you see things as they really are, it seems impossible that it's true. How could it be true? I want to do exactly what God wants? I have a new heart that beats only for him? Yet, that's exactly what Jesus says.

So here's your opportunity today…

As you run into situations, and you ask yourself, "Who am I, what do I really want…what is it that I really want out of my life?" Take a look at the facts… choose to believe God. Take him at his word, because he's telling the truth. You DO want to do exactly what he wants. That's who you are. Now go live out what you truly want. Live out your hearts deepest desire.

Choose Your Master

Romans 6:12-14

Why not sin? We're continuing with this question. A couple of days ago you listed some of the reasons you use NOT to sin...um...none of which worked very well.

Review what the Bible says. Why not remain in sin? Why not remain under that old system the one where you draw the line, and you can't help but want to jump it, even though it brings more grace into your life?

The answer is, you died to that...that's not who you are. The answer to that question is because you've risen with Christ...that IS who you are. The answer is, your old self was crucified. The answer to that is because you have died and been freed from sin. The answer to that is because you live with Christ...you actually want to do what God wants, just like Jesus wants.

There's one more answer!

The final answer we pick up in verse 12...it says, "Therefore do not let sin reign in your mortal body so that you obey its evil desires. Do not offer the parts of your body to sin, as instruments of wickedness, but rather offer yourselves to God…"

Take note of what it says here "…offer the parts of your body…"

You see, your heart, your spirit, the person you are has already been given to Christ…it's already been given to God. You put your faith in him, and therefore he's made that brand new. But you still have that choice. And it would just be foolish, wouldn't it, to offer my body to someone who's really my enemy?

"…but rather offer yourselves to God as those who have been brought from death to life…offer the parts of your body to him as instruments of righteousness."

On a day-to-day basis, on a moment by moment basis, we have a choice to make. The choice isn't who are we going to be…the choice isn't who are we…that's already been settled. The choice is, Am I going to trust what God says about me, and therefore offer my body…offer my hands, and my eyes, and my nose, and my brain, and my feet…am I going to offer them to God who I belong to, who is one with me, who is no longer at war with me, who has given me all of this incredible grace? Or am I going to believe that all of what he said about me just isn't true.

I am God's so I want to use body, mind and soul to give my best to my boss or I am like everyone else so I want to use my body, mind and soul to get by on the least amount of effort as possible. I will use my body to serve me.

I am God's so I want to use my eyes and words to honor that woman as special and beautiful. Or I am a red blooded American man so I want to use my eyes and mind to use that woman's beauty to feed my lust for sexual gratification.

Practice that today. As you run into situations…

don't ask yourself do I want to do this. Ask yourself...
Who am I...and who do I want to offer my body to?

The Box Disappears - More Grace

Romans 6:14

We're still going with that question...yes!

Why not remain in the sin? Why not remain in a place where we are controlled by sin, and therefore, we continue to get more and more grace from God?

We've been given quite a few amazing answers to that question so far, and all of them are incredibly true and they are ours to grasp hold of and hold on to with all of our might.

But in verse 14 of chapter 6, Paul really summarizes the whole thing, and he makes this incredible, amazing statement. Yes, another one! Why not sin?

"For the sin (that thing which causes you to jump the line when a line is drawn in the sand) shall not be your master..."

How can that be? How could it be that it will no longer be my master? I mean, from the day I was born, from the time my parents first told me "no"...I have struggled with and fought with this part of me that just wants to do what I want to do, and even though it's gotten me into great trouble, and causes great pain in my life, I can't seem to overcome it! It's always there with me...how could it not be my master?

"...because you are not under law..."

Remember what we learned about the sin? We learned that if you bring the law along...draw the line in the sand...it comes to life and it has power. BUT "...you are not under law, but under grace."

What does that mean....exactly! Draw a box on this page, and put yourself inside of that box. The sides of that box are very personal for each one of us because it's based on what WE THINK God demands of us, the things WE THINK that God says. "If you do this, as long a you don't do the other thing, as long as you keep this in order, and produce this, then I'll be pleased with you...we'll have a relationship. You'll get my grace...you'll get good things in your life." You, being a good Christian person, fill in the blank. What things are written on the sides of your box?

But as unbelievable as it is, once you put your faith in Christ, THERE IS NO BOX, there is no law...which means none of your sins are written down...none of your transgressions are recorded. Christ died to the law, he totally fulfilled it. Every sin...every transgression...all of them...been paid for. You're not under that law. You're under grace. The more you sin, the more grace you get. Gone! Finished! Your relationship to God is no longer based on what you do or what you produce, or how well you do it. It's solely based upon grace. It's a gift. It's going to be there no matter what you live like...no matter what you do.

So here's the principle.

Understand this...grab a hold of this. THE SIN dies. It DOESN'T HAVE POWER IN YOUR LIFE. When you believe that this is true, when you look at the circumstances, look at what God says is true, and you choose what God says is true, then THE SIN will not be your master.

And Paul is saying that you can commit acts of sin over and over and over again, but you're not under law. It's never going to be written down. And we know that this is what it teaches because the very next question that Paul asked is, "What then, shall we sin...?"

And this time he doesn't say, "THE SIN"... he says SIN...commit acts of sin. Is it ok? We're not under law, we're under grace.

We'll talk about that tomorrow.

Why Not Sin?

Romans 6:15

So… What's it like to live outside of the box?

What's it like to realize that because of God's grace… because we stand in grace…because he has justified us…because he has made us right with him…because he has bought us and paid for all of our sin…because he has satisfied all of God's wrath, that we now are at peace with God, regardless of how well we live up to the standard. Our sins are never again written down from this day forward. What's it like to know that in any and every situation you can turn to God at any time because the relationship he has with you is pure and right and good. It seems pretty unbelievable, huh?

AND it also leads to the next question…the question that Paul asks in verse 15…

"What, then? Shall we sin because we are not under law, but under grace? By no means"

Now the reason we know that our interpretation in verse 14 is right…correct…is because it leads us to ask this very question that Paul asked. And his answer is, "BY NO MEANS!"

And you know why. It's really simple…he's been

saying again and again and again! The answer to the question "Why not sin?"…the question "Who are we?"…the question "Do we belong to Adam…are we who we were when we were born…or do we belong to Jesus? What's the answer? The answer is…because THAT'S NOT WHO WE ARE!

Read verse 17.

"But thanks be to God that though you used to be slaves to sin, you wholeheartedly obeyed the form of teaching to which you were entrusted. You have been set free from sin, and have become slaves of righteousness." Why not commit acts of sin? THAT'S NOT WHO YOU ARE!

It's a very simple principle, don't you think? Why would you offer your bodies to that which brings death and destruction if that's not who you are?

And that's the next reason Paul gives us for not committing acts of sin. Sin only leads to destruction, and, really, I can't think of a single sin I've ever committed that I'm proud of, can you?

As a matter of fact, do that!

Can you think of any sin that you've ever committed, that you're like, "Man, I'm glad I did that… I'm really proud of that…That was a good thing to do. As I look back on what I did and had to do it all over again, I'd do it just like that again." NO!! Why? It's because it brings shame, and it brings destruction, and it brings hurt…and in the long run, it never helps. It always brings death.

Paul wraps it all up like this…

"For the wages of sin is death…"

Why not sin? It only produces destruction and hurt…in our relationships, in our job, in our personal lives, in our spirit, in our heart…

82

"...but the gift of God is eternal life in Jesus Christ our Lord."

ETERNAL LIFE!

It doesn't just mean life that lives forever. It means that I'm actually, really alive! It means that when I get up in the morning I know that I have purpose, and my life counts, and it matters. Why? I have a relationship with God that's pure and right and good. I'm going to give my life, I'm going to give my body, I'm going to give whatever years I have left to REALLY LIVING! That's what I was created for. THAT"S being alive! That's reversing what happened to Adam when he died.

Instead of living THAT way, we're going to live a whole NEW way.

Because you're alive, because you are no longer about the business of proving your self or accumulating stuff to give yourself meaning, what do you want to do with the rest of your life?

Grace Stories

It's your turn to write, create, communicate!

Take a few minutes to write where you are on the journey of grace. It may be a story, picture, formula, proverb or even a game you create. For those of you who might be tempted to skip this page, don't skip it! Spend time thinking about what God is doing in your life based on what you're learning.

Living a New Way

Romans 7:6

"But now, by dying to what once bound us, we have been released from the law so that we serve in the new way of the Spirit not the old way of the written code."

We know the old way of the written code. It's the box. It's the law...the life of proving, earning and hiding. But this new way of the written code is strange to us. It's not a life without right or wrong. It's a relationship, and intimate relationship based on grace. Grace is   deserving NOTHING but being given EVERYTHING.

In this new relationship the question is not what can I get away with? The question is not "Why can't I...?" The question is, What is the best thing to do? What will show the most love? What will bring the best results? What will heal the heart, build trust? The question is not, "How do I get God's love and blessing?" The question is, now that my life is secure in Christ, how do I use my time and talents to make a difference? The question is not who am I? The question is, now that I know who I am how do I live that out on a day-to-day basis?

The answer?

To walk in the spirit is to trust Jesus for what is TRUE, for WHO YOU ARE and for the POWER to live out this new life. It is looking forward to loving what is right and knowing that WE ARE FREE from the past.

This is the basis of everything we are going to talk about for the rest of our journey.

So...spend some time meditating on what the difference is between serving the law versus serving the Spirit.

Try this: When you're making a decision, consider these factors:

1. What does the Bible say?
2. If God is on my side, what is there to fear?
3. What will bring about what I (really want. (Remember...you love God's way!)
4. If I fail, does it change who God has made me to be?

Putting Others in the Box

Romans 7:9-12

Today instead of looking at how people try to put us in the box, or we put ourselves inside the box as we relate to God, we're going to take a look at how often we try to put other people in the box.

In the context of our close relationships we often try to get them to understand us, get them to see what is right. What we're really trying to do is create a box around their lives. We draw a line and say, "Now look…if you step over this line, that's the wrong thing to do." So here's what it sounds like between a husband and wife…This could be true about any issue, spending money, sex, use of time, hobbies just about anything. Husband: I read today that it is natural for a woman to want to take care of her husband. I can see how it would really help our marriage if you would take better care of me. Wife: I read today that a good man brings home enough to live on, helps out with the kids, gives his wife a few hours to be with her friends and takes out the garbage. If you changed I just might want to take care of you. Can you see how each person tries to get the other one to change by focusing on the behavior that would make their spouse a better person. They are building the box in hopes it will keep them in.

We see the same kind of relationship happen with co-workers, in the office or wherever, and there's this atmosphere of people trying to put everybody else inside a box. There's this competition to see who can be the most right, or we're always looking for someone else who does something wrong so we can bring them up short, this was wrong and that was wrong...kind of get the upper hand..."I'm the one who is the most right..." What we're doing is, we're creating boxes... we're putting people under the law. And we think... "If I can just get the box built around them tight enough, they'll behave the way I want them to behave, right?

Really, we see it most clearly with children. The truth is, from 0-9 years old, it's actually a good thing to teach a child by the law...it's very good to teach that child, "If you touch that stove, you are going to get hurt...It's hot...don't touch the stove." It's very good to teach them, "If you go into that road, there's going to be a painful application to your bottom...don't go into the road!" They need to understand that they are not the center of the world... they need to understand that there are laws, there are rules, there are ways to live that are good and right. God is the righteous and good judge.

Ah...but then they grow up! And you'll notice, when a child gets to be anywhere from 11 to 19, maybe even quite a bit younger than that, before your very eyes, you'll see these sweet, little, darling children will all of a sudden become rebellious. What is that? What's going on in their lives?

88

What's going on in their lives is exactly what's explained in Romans 7:9-14

"Once I was alive apart from the law; but when the commandment came sin sprang alive and I died. I found that the very commandment that was intended to bring life actually brought death."

See…as we grow up…we don't do well inside of the box! And the thing is, there's no way we can build relationships if we're only dealing with THE BOX. So what does the goal need to be? The goal in all of our relationships is, STOP RELATING TO PEOPLE BASED ON THE BOX. Begin to relate to people based on love, and grace and forgiveness. Begin to relate to people the way God relates to us. If we begin to look at life this way, it will become really, really clear why people act the way they do. It will also be really clear how much God's grace and love is needed in people's lives.

I am not saying that you don't have rules or don't teach the truth. What changes is that I don't relate to you based on trying to change your behavior but honesty, faith, love and grace. Of course this means that others may choose not to connect with us. In the same way many choose not to connect with God.

Try that out today…

As you go through your day…your daily activities… just try that on for size. Instead of focusing on what you ought NOT to do, begin to ask yourself… "If this is who I am…if this is who God says I am, then what do I want to do today? As I enjoy this relationship with God, what do I want to do?"

Listen to him. Believe him. And have a great day!

Why Do I Still Sin?

Romans 7:14-25

The Bible has painted a PRETTY INCREDIBLE picture so far!

We've gone from being under God's wrath, to being made right with God, to all of our sins being paid for, to God's wrath being satisfied, to the point where, no matter whether we sin or not, God gives us more grace. We're at peace with God. We stand in an amazing place of grace. His power and his spirit live within us… we are alive the way that Christ is alive. What an incredible position God has put us in!

And yet, what do our day-to-day lives look like? Do our day-to-day lives look any different than they did before we came to Christ? They have changed considerably but do they look like what we have learned up to this point? We often find ourselves doing the same things…lying about the same things…hiding the same things…being afraid of the same things.

So that really brings up yet another question! Yikes!

If all of these great things are true, and all of this is true of me, then why do I still sin? Why am I still hurting people around me? Why am I not able to control myself and do what I'm so suppose to do?

Paul says there's a reason for that. Sure am glad that we're finding reasons, aren't you?

So here's the reason…here's what he says. Your spirit, your heart, the core of who you are, has been redeemed…it has been saved…it's been changed. BUT the body you live in still has sin in it. Your mind has old ways of thinking.

Remember…way back in chapter three it said that our minds were worthless…unusable? Well, our bodies also have selfishness and lusts…and all of that is still there…in our bodies.

It says in Romans 7:14, "We know that the law is spiritual; but I am unspiritual, sold as a slave to sin. I do not understand what I do. For what I want to do I do not do, but what I hate to do. And if I do what I do not want to do, I agree that the law is good. As it is, it is no longer I myself who do it, but it is sin living in me."

THERE IT IS! Did you see it? It's sin living in me! It's not that our bodies are sinful, it's not that our bodies are evil, it's that sin lives within us. It can't be changed. It can't be improved. It can't be cleaned up.

So this really brings us to a day-to-day decision making process.

Go back and read Romans 3:21-26. Then read Romans 6:10 & 11. Reread the things that God says about you.

Now wait a minute…who am I REALLY!…and what is this battle that I'm facing?

Over the next couple of days we're going to learning about the battle. As we do, keep asking…

Can I really trust God for what he says…who he says I am?

Defining the War
Law vs. Grace

Romans 7:14-25

For years, as I was growing up I would hear people speak, or I would read about people in books, and they would talk about this incredible love they had for God...this incredible passion they had for other people, for the world, for being able to do what was right... help the needy. And I wanted to be just like that...I always tried to have that passion. I always tried to work on my heart to be that kind of person. I wanted that so badly.

So I would pray for it...I would mentally beat up on myself for falling short. One way or another I was going to be just like those people. I would strongly commit that I was going to be that kind of person, and yet I found that every time I did, it just didn't work. It wasn't strong enough. It wasn't big enough. It was never acceptable.

As I finished my schooling and was about to go into the ministry, I was asked myself...How can I possibly go into the ministry if I don't have the kind of heart that I need to have. Then I discovered this passage...it was in Romans 7:21…

"So I find this law at work: When I want to do good, evil is right there with me."

Are you saying what I was saying? THAT'S MY LIFE! Well, this was also Paul's life. He was struggling with sin.

Then he says the most amazing thing! Yes… ANOTHER amazing thing!

"For in my inner being I delight in God's law…"

He wasn't working at it…he wasn't working at having this happen. This was true of him! What he discovered, as you will, is that you can't change your own heart…your heart is what it is. Only God can change your heart. And his promise is that when you put your faith in his Son…when you put your faith in Jesus…he gives you a new heart! He gives you a heart that always delights in his law. Hear this! You DO want to do what God wants. That IS who you are.

"…but I see another law…" (or another principle) "… at work in the members of my body, waging war against the law of my mind and making me a prisoner of the law of sin…"

So there it is…there's the bottom line of the problem. That is how our lives are, isn't it? It's this great strug-gle…this great battle that we have between really wanting to do what God wants us to and what we ac-tually end up doing.

Paul says there are two players in this war. The first player is the law of grace…the law of the spirit of life which says…YOU ARE A NEW PERSON. It says, "I do delight in God's law…I am a new person…I do want to serve God…I do want to do the right thing."

Then there is that second player…the law of the prisoner of sin which says, "No, you are not that

93

person, and I can prove it. Look at the way you live?" It says, "Look...don't cross this line...if you cross this line then you don't love God. You've GOT TO PROVE that you love God. You've got to prove it by staying inside of the box and living inside of the box. You've got to prove it...."

And then we discover grace....

We're so free and we're like, "I'll never go back...I'll always live this way! I want to live this way forever!"

Understand this...

The flesh is always drawing us back. It NEVER wants to change. It's always drawing us back to living as though I have to become pleasing to God ...he has to be contented...sacrifices have to be given in some way so he can be happy with me....and then he can be a part of my life and bless me... It's that vicious, flesh-cycle all over again. BUT what we've discovered, again and again and again...Who am I?

The Bible says, if you are a believer, you love God with all of your heart, and the flesh hurls it's venom and says, "Oh no you don't..." Who will you believe? Day by day, minute by minute, who will you trust?

Write out the two players who are pulling on you.

Write out what they are pulling on you to believe and do.

Who Will Rescue Me?

Romans 7:14-25

Anger, overspending, procrastination, decision making, addiction...emotional problems...mental problems...physical problems...

We are constantly going to seminars, listening to talk shows, the news, reading the books...it's all about changing your behavior...the quick "how-to" or "tips that will change your life." How do we change? How does someone change?

But when Paul asked the same question...he discovered THE LIFE CHANGING ANSWER. He discovered God's grace. It is the "end all" answer of all time!

He knows God's grace, he knows he's been forgiven, he knows who he is...he's a new person, he knows he stands in grace, he has peace with God, he has been made right with God.

So what's the problem?

He still struggles with sin! He understands that sin lives within him. He understands, better than anybody, the two wars that are at work. The one war drawing him back to living under the law, where sin can have power...the other saying, "No, you're free! You're free! All you have to do is trust what God has to say...trust what God says about you!"

Oh, he's looking at his life...looking at the way he lives, what he does, what he says, what he acts like, his attitudes. Believe me...he's seeing his flesh for what it is, and with a deep groan he asks...

"What a wretched man I am! WHO WILL RESCUE ME from this body of death? (7:24)

If you're struggling just as Paul was, you're definitely feeling his desperation. And you want him to feel better. But the answer is not, "Oh no, no, no... you're not bad...that's not true!" No! Paul is being really realistic. He's taken a good look at his life, and he knows there must be something better.

Looking at my own life...what I know to be true. I know what is right. I've been given this incredible forgiveness, and yet, on a day-to-day basis, day in and day out, as I make decisions, I see my wretchedness. I'm not comparing myself to anybody else. All I have to do is compare myself to what God has called me to... what he's made me to be on the inside. That's when it becomes really clear that I'm a wretched man.

So who will save me from this body of death? How do I change? How do I get out of this? How do I become on the outside, the person I am on the inside?

This is amazing, BUT TRUE! Ready?

The answer is NOT to work harder at it...

The answer is NOT commitments...

It's NOT to read the Bible more or study the Bible more...

It's NOT to go to a seminar, or go to church more...

It's NONE OF THOSE THINGS!

The answer is…

"Thanks be to God – THROUGH JESUS CHRIST OUR LORD!"

Jesus is responsible! He says, "I'll take on the responsibility…I will rescue you from your sinfulness…BRING IT ON!!!

How about that?

So if I'm lazy, then I admit that to Christ. I say, "Jesus, I want you to do whatever it takes to get rid of that." And he takes that responsibility. I can trust him with that. Then I follow him. I take whatever step he is leading me to take. I always have the power to take the first step. But it takes trust in Jesus because we can rarely see where the next five steps will lead.

Why don't you take the things that you want to see changed in your life, trust Christ, and ask him? Just say, "Hey, Jesus I know that you're going to take that on." That's his responsibility to deal with it. Our responsibility is simply to trust him…to follow him.

No Condemnation

Romans 8:1

Are you having a good day? How about a good week? What's your success rate been this week? How are you doing at living out the person God has created you to be? How are you doing with sin and righteousness and goodness? How are you doing at pouring your life into things that count and into purposeful things versus the selfishness, the bad attitude, the temper tantrums, or maybe just blahs...the feelings of failure...the struggle with inadequacy? How are you doing?

If you're having a bad week, and maybe you're not... maybe you're great...you're on top of the world, but you remember back to one of those other weeks...times you know will happen again, and ask yourself, "I wonder what God thinks of me right now?" You know what I'm talking about. The times when you're like, "Man, the way I'm acting...the way I'm living, God must be...he must be just shaking his head at me"

That's what Paul was saying yesterday. "What a wretched man I am!" He says, "Who's going to rescue me?" And then there was that breath of relief...Jesus is going to rescue me.

At the end of verse 25 he says, "So then I myself in my mind am a slave to God's law, but in the sinful nature, a slave to the law of sin." I'm struggling! Well, he says, here's the joy...here's the answer...here's the peace...

"Therefore, there is now no condemnation for those who are in Christ Jesus..."

WOW! What a statement! No condemnation means no disgust, no disappointment, no shaking his head... that's right! NONE! ZERO! ZIP!

"...because, through Jesus Christ the law of the spirit of life SET ME FREE from the law of sin and death."

There it is again! That war! And Paul wants you to know that when you're in the middle of that struggle, GOD DOESN'T CONDEMN YOU! If he did, you'd be back under the law. BUT HE DOESN'T! Why? Jesus paid it all. All that stuff you think he's frustrated with, all that stuff you think he's disappointed with. Jesus paid for ALL of that. And God is INCREDIBLY PLEASED with you.

Do you treat other people that way? I mean, as you interact with other people who are struggling with sin, they're not living the way you think they should...are you known as the person who condemns, who judges? Are you the person who rolls the eyes, shakes the head, that big sigh...? Maybe that's because you think that God looks at YOU that way.

Track the people you are frustrated with in your life. Then compare your attitude toward them with God's graceful attitude toward you. See what it does to your attitude.

Your Turn

It's your turn to write, create, communicate!

Take a few minutes to write where you are on the journey of grace. It may be a story, picture, formula, proverb or even a game you create. For those of you who might be tempted to skip this page, don't skip it! Spend time thinking about what God is doing in your life based on what you're learning.

Flesh Is a Formidable Enemy

Romans 8:5-8

I just went to the refrigerator and did one of my favorite things. I got out a bottle of whipped cream, and turned it upside down, and sprayed it in my mouth. Good stuff!

Now, I promised myself that I was just going to do it that ONE time, but as always, once I get a taste for it, I always have to do it just a few more times.

That's the way it is with most things, really. All things in the flesh, are like that, doesn't matter if it's big or small. We want to control it. We want to try it...just do a little bit. It might be lust for sexual things... "I'm just going to look a little bit...maybe just a little bit further." Instead of satisfying it, we end up creating this incredible passion or hunger for more. "I'm just going to buy a few things, and once I get these things I'll be satisfied..." But it never does...it always wants more. Just about any sin in our lives is just like that...it's never satisfied...it wants a little bit more.

Ok...so...we've become new persons. Now how do we bring our bodies to life? How is Jesus going to do that? How is he going to rescue us from the sins that destroy our lives, and ruin our relationships?

Paul starts off by telling us what the enemy is like, and that's what our focus is about today. And believe me…this is really clear!

"Those who live according to the sinful nature have their minds set on what that nature desires; but those who live in accordance with the Spirit have their minds set on what the Spirit desires. The mind of sinful man…" and take note of this…this is very clear… "The mind of the sinful man is death, but the mind controlled by the Spirit is life and peace; the sinful mind is hostile to God…" that means it's an enemy of God…it hates God! "It does not submit to God's law, NOR CAN IT DO SO. Those controlled by the sinful nature cannot please God."

WOW! What a clear, clear picture!

As we're living life, we have this great desire to maybe hang on to what we have…maybe improve it, somehow…that's all. Ok…so maybe my language is not what God wants…but maybe I can improve it. Maybe my thought life is not right where it needs to be, but certainly, I can improve that. That's what I want to do. We keep trying and trying…trying to improve our sinful natures. We try to be less lustful…less selfish…less hurtful… less of a procrastinator. We just try to dial them down…be better…

The Bible is very clear. YOU CAN'T IMPROVE! You're not going to overcome the weaknesses in your life. You're not going to overcome these sins in your life by dialing them down. It's never going to be one little step at a time…one little step at a time. Why? It's because they will never, ever, ever, EVER submit to God's law. They hate God.

So...let's make a commitment together.

Let's quit trying. Let's quit trying to do it.

We're going to find out tomorrow...well....if we're not going to dial it down, then what ARE we going to do with it?

God's Spirit Alive in My Spirit Together Fighting the Flesh

Romans 8:9-13

What a wretched man I am…Who's going to rescue me?

We're still trying desperately to answer that question! This looks impossible! It seems impossible that I'll ever, ever, actually change!

I want to give you a bit of encouragement today as we move on, and we take a look at the "players" in the battle to overcome the sin that's in our lives…of actually LIVING OUT who we are on the inside.

So let's start right in…

In Romans 8:9 it says, "You, however, are controlled not by the sinful nature but by the Spirit, if the Spirit of God lives in you. And if anyone does not have the Spirit of Christ, he does not belong to Christ."

So let's be introduced…

There are really three players…there's your flesh, there's your spirit, and there's God's spirit. And the principle Paul really wants you to understand is this… Your spirit and God's Spirit are one. They are working together to defeat your flesh.

He says it even stronger…

104

"And if the Spirit of him who raised Jesus from the dead is living in you, he who raised Christ from the dead will also give life to your mortal bodies…"

That very same Spirit that overcame all of your sin… everything you've ever done, thought, EVERYTHING…was poured out on Christ. He became sin for us, and yet, the Spirit of God was powerful enough to overcome that, and bring Jesus back to life. Well…that same Spirit is going to give life to your mortal bodies, through his Spirit who lives in you.

So…as you approach that problem…as you approach that struggle…the question is not, "God…are you on my side? GOD IS ALWAYS ON YOUR SIDE! He lives within you. And the question is NOT "Am I on God's side?" Yes! A hundred times YES! In your inner being…at the core of who you are…YOU ARE EXACTLY WHAT GOD WANTS!

The question is…Can you believe it?

When you look at the circumstances, just like Abraham did, and it looks like it's impossible…you're as good as dead. But when you look at God's word…it says your alive! You're a slave to righteousness. This flesh that you're struggling with is not what you want. You want to love that wife of yours with the passion, courage and strength of a gentle warrior. You want to love and care for and sacrifice for your kids. You want to do whatever it takes to become a wise person, to know how to handle situations. You want to be the man at work that can be trusted. You want to be the leader in your community because of the way you sacrifice for others and love others around you.

Know this today…your spirit and God's Spirit are on the same side.

Try this: As you face struggles to do the right thing, first, choose who you're going to believe, Jesus or your feelings. That tells you who you are and what you truly want to do. "I want to get up and take care of the baby crying before she wakes up my wife." After you know who you are, be yourself, act on the truth, not your feelings.

How Do I Put to Death the Misdeeds of the Flesh?

Romans 8:13

Remember, as a child, sitting in class at school, and the teacher's saying, "Ok...this is what we're going to do today, we're working on this big project, this is how we're going to do it, and this is what we're going to do, and this is what's going to happen," and you're just jumping in your seat and you keep raising your hand, "Teacher...teacher...But what do I do? What do I do? What's my role? What's my part? Tell me what to do."

The question is still, "How do I change? How do I overcome the sin that's ruining my life and destroying my life? What do I do? Tell me what to do.

God says...This is how...

The foundation is GRACE. He says, "The reason you have a relationship with me is because of what I have done for you. I don't condemn you any longer because of what my son paid...for you. My Spirit actually LIVES WITHIN YOU, and is on your side.

"Good...good...good...good...great...now what do I do...What's my role?

Romans 8:12 says your role is not to focus on what

you're NOT to do...your role is NOT to focus on your sinful nature...NOT to focus on the flesh. Your role is to focus on the Spirit, who you are, and where you're headed. Look FORWARD in your life. Check it out...

"Therefore, brothers, we have an obligation – but it is not to the sinful nature, to live according to it. For if you live according to the sinful nature, you will die..."

That word "obligation" is an interesting word...it's like you owe something. We don't owe the sinful nature anything. We don't need to give it another thought. We don't need to excuse it, we don't need to nurture it, we don't need to think about how we're going to destroy it or what we're going to do to it, or how I'm going to manage it. If we're trying to manage the sinful nature, we're paying WAY too much attention to it. Paul says...don't do that...or you're going to die.

"...but if by the Spirit you put to death the misdeeds of the body, you will live..."

It's very important that you catch those words..."by the Spirit" What does that mean? What does it mean to do it "by the Spirit?"

"To put to death the misdeeds of the body" It's pretty simple...kill it!

If it's lust...it's not that we control lust...it's not that we manage lust...it's that we kill it! No more! Shut it down! Nip it in the bud! If we're talking about greed... kill it...cut it off! We can't be partially greedy, either. Or if it's selfishness, it's not that we can be just a little bit selfish or just LESS selfish. No! We cut it off!

Well...that seems kind of drastic, don't you think?

Nope! If it says to do it by the Spirit, then that's what we do. We trust what the Spirit says...and we act on what the Spirit says. He knows what he's doing!

You were under God's wrath because there was no righteousness in you whatsoever. The Spirit says, "I am putting righteousness into you. You're either going to choose to live one way or the other. Whatever it is... whatever it's about...you're either going to choose to get rid of it and turn your life over to God and say, "Ok...I'm going to follow the Spirit. I know where I'm headed."

The Spirit just wants to lead you to life. Grab hold... look forward... and say, "That's what I want to do...I want to be that person. I want to be that very person that God has made me to be. I want to live that out. But I can't do that and lust at the same time, so, I'm going to get rid of the lust. I can't be selfish and be the mother that God has created me to be in the inside. So, I'm going to get rid of the selfishness. I can't love my wife and be worried about my career and my status at the same time, so I've got to put that aside. Why? It's because of who I am. I belong to Christ. I want what God wants.

As we do that, amazing things happen...the Spirit of God takes that same body that was used to hurt, the same tongue that was used to cut, and he uses it to heal, as he replaces your thoughts, and your attitudes, and your actions, with those of Christ.

I Call Him Daddy

Romans 8:14-16

When you close your eyes and you envision what your relationship with God is like, what do you see? Do you see an old grandfather who is nice and kind, and sort of looks the other way when you do wrong. Do you see a judge with a big, long, flowing beard, and with a strong staff in his arm, he judges every little thing and never lets anything by? Who is it that you see? What does your relationship to the Father...the creator of this universe...look like?

Today, as a part of our study of grace, we come to the best part! We're going to see why it is that we can put to death the deeds of the body...why we can throw away the old life and trust the new life. It's all wrapped up in this relationship that we now have. Read, as Paul describes it...

"...because those who are led by the Spirit of God are sons of God. For you did not receive a spirit that makes you a slave again to fear..."

WOW! No more fear!

From this moment on, as a believer, any time you interact with God and you're afraid of him, you think he's against you, you think you can't talk to him, you don't want to be with him, you don't want to be around him...well...that's slavery, and Paul says YOU'RE FREE OF THAT!

"... but you received the Spirit of sonship. And by him we cry, Abba, Father."

It's daddy! He's daddy!

"Abba" is the word that we would use for daddy... it's endearing. Whatever word you use in your family...dad...pop...it may even be father. It's the word that you use when you call your dad, and you know you're calling the man who always puts you first...the man who protects, and cares, and does right for you. That is the relationship that you have with God the father. Unfortunately you may have never experienced this with your father, but only dreamed of it. Now you can experience it.

This very moment, through the day today, every single day, 24/7, in every situation, you can know beyond a shadow of a doubt that God is on your side. He's your daddy.

What's your question? Do you want to know if it's true for everyone?

The answer is, no.

It's only true for those who stand in grace. It's only true for those who've accepted this incredible gift that he has for you.

Try This: As you're following the spirit today and living this new life, undoubtedly sin will rear its ugly head. The usual reaction is to try and fight it alone. Get clean and then go talk to God. Today in the middle of the battle tell God everything you're going through. Ask for his help in the battle.

God Brings His Promise into My Life

Romans 8:28-30

"Man... I wish God would just come down here and tell me exactly what he's doing in my life. I wish he'd just tell me exactly what's going on here...why are these things happening? What's he up to? What's going on? Have you ever thought that?

These next verses from Paul are great because that's exactly what God does! He makes us an incredible promise. He tells us just exactly how he's using everything that happens in our lives... to make us like his Son. Pretty cool!

Ok...I'm waiting...on with it!

What is God doing in my life? How is he working to help me become on the outside the person I've become on the inside?

It starts with the FACT that God is working to make you JUST LIKE HIS SON!

Now, if you don't know who Jesus is, and you don't know what he's like, then this wouldn't be such a big deal to you. But if you have, then Jesus is the person that you always really wanted to be. He's the person who does the right thing, the wise thing, the strong thing, the powerful thing, the helpful and courageous thing all the time. He's the person who walks into a war and gives his life for others. He's the one who walks into a room and gives away to those in need, the way they need it. He's the one who walk into a room and says the right things that bring healing. He's the one who walks into a room and says the right things that confront evil and stops it in its tracks. THAT'S WHO HE IS!

All the glory that we desire, all of the completeness, all the joy and the peace and the strength that we desire...that's who he is. That's what his life is like every day.

And THAT"S what God's doing in your life. He is trying to turn you into that person.

"For we know that in all things God works for the good of those who love him."

Throughout this whole day, from this day forward, you can know this...absolutely everything...good, bad, upside down, inside out, EVERYTHING...God wants to use it for YOUR good to make YOU like him.

"...for those who love him, who have been called according to his purpose. For those God foreknew he also predestined to be conformed to the likeness of his Son." (8:28)

That's the goal!

When your neighbor does something that irritates you, God wants to use that to make you like his Son. When someone cuts you off in traffic, God wants to make you like his Son. When you make really bad decisions and you end up being in financial trouble, or somebody else makes bad decisions, and you end up being in financial trouble, God wants to use that to

113

make you like his Son.

He's ALWAYS working to make you on the outside, who he's made you to be on the inside.

Try this: Approach today like you're going to work out. When you work out you put up with the pain because you know it is going to make you stronger, more fit, toned. The hotter the burn the more we are going to get out of it. That is how we can live on a day–to-day basis. The person at the DMV may think they are making life tough for me, but I know that God is using this to make me like him. My kids may think they are pushing my buttons but I know that God is using this to make me like him. The harder others push on me the better person I am becoming. It is a win-win.

What Is Jesus Doing Right Now?

Romans 8:34

Wouldn't you like to know what Jesus is doing right now...this very minute? Have you ever wondered? Sometimes you hear people say, "Wait till you hear what Jesus did today. Jesus did this, and Jesus did that. This happened because of Jesus. And you're like... "Wait just minute! How do you know that Jesus did that?"

Well, there actually is something that we can know that Jesus is doing...right now. And that's what we're going to talk about today.

Many times you'll hear these words...Jesus talked to me...or he spoke to me. The Bible really says that it's absolutely true. The Spirit really does speak to us...all the time.

Ok, listen...this can be a bit confusing...I mean, is this one person, or three people?

It's three in one....and no...I can't explain it...but it's how the Bible talks, it's what it says, it's how it says it works out, and so that's what I believe, and that's what I trust.

Ok...What is Jesus doing...right now?

Paul wraps everything up with this incredible explanation of the Gospel. We've seen how good God is. God is so good that he would take those who are his enemies...those who are against him...who rebel against him...and always choose to go the other way...and who have been hurtful and destructive...and he offers them his grace. He pays the penalty for them...to the point that they could not just get out of trouble, but they could become like him...they could have the righteousness that he has. It's just too good to be true!

And now we've understood that we stand in grace, and that our role is to trust him, and our role is to say YES to the spirit which leads to saying NO to sin...simply say, NO... because that's not who we are.

What's Jesus doing? Right now?

Romans 8:34 says, "Who is he that condemns?"

There are a lot of voices that condemn us. It may be the voice of your parents. It may be the voice of your boss. It may be your inner voice. There are a lot of voices that say, "You're an idiot...you're no good... you're not good enough...you didn't make it...you don't measure up...you don't please..."

Remember the very question we started with? Is God 100% pleased with you?

Here's his answer...

"Who is he that condemns? Christ Jesus, who died - more than that, who was raised to life – is at the right hand of God and is also interceding for us."

From other passages in the Bible we know that Satan actually goes to heaven and he says, "Look...look what that person is doing wrong. And look what that other person is doing wrong. They don't deserve to go to heaven. They claim to be part of your family, but look...look what they're doing."

And Jesus is at the right hand of the Father saying, No, no, no, no, no...I paid for that! No...I rose from the dead and defeated that...he's mine! He belongs to me...he is good enough...I am pleased with him... 100%

Wow! I mean, right now...even as you're reading this, that's exactly what Jesus is doing on your behalf.

As you live your life today, and as you hear those voices, think. Are those voices trustworthy, or is Jesus voice trustworthy? And if you ever think you hear Jesus condemning you...IT'S NOT TRUE!

The choice is...which voice am I going to believe?

Who Is the Winner?

Romans 8:35-39

Who's the winner? Who's going to win? Am I going to win? Am I going to make it? Does my life count? Does my life matter? Who's the winner? Who gets away with it? Do they get away with it? Am I going to get away with it? We're really concerned about who wins in the end.

From the very beginning, in taking this journey together, we saw that NO ONE WAS GOING TO GET AWAY WITH ANYTHING. Everyone will answer to God.

And for those who choose God's grace…for those who accept his gift, and no longer trust in anything but the promise of God, we've seen the incredible promises that he's given of forgiveness and righteousness and purity and victory over sin and eternal life.

As we come to the end, are you still looking at your life and saying, "Aw, but look at my life…life doesn't look like that at all…I mean…look at the struggle I'm having here, and the financial struggles, the emotional struggles…look at my life…even my struggle with

118

sin..."

Listen. Just listen. Read this and really listen to what it's saying...

"Who shall separate us from the love of Christ? Shall trouble or hardship or persecution or famine or nakedness or danger or sword? As it is written, for your sake we face death all day long; we are considered as sheep to be   slaughtered. NO, in all of these things we are more than conquerors through him who loved us."

You see...the final question is...Who am I and who am I going to be for eternity?

Right NOW I'm still in the war zone. Right NOW I'm still struggling...but I know that God's love is ALWAYS there for me. It's not based on what I do...it's based on his grace. I'm going to receive the promise of God because he gave it to me by his grace.
Finish it up...What does the rest say? You don't want to miss a thing!

"For I am convinced that neither death nor life, neither angels nor demons, neither the present nor the future, nor any powers, neither height nor depth, nor anything else in all creation, will be able to separate us from the love of God that is in Christ Jesus our Lord."

You can have incredible confidence in who you are. Although it may not look like you are who God says you are, he promises...that's who you are. He promises he will make you like his Son in the end. No matter what the obstacle is, no matter how bad it looks and how ugly it looks, you can live with full confidence that you belong to God, and that he is making you to be like his Son. That's a life worth living...that's a   purpose that lasts for eternity.

Try this: Make a list of everything you are trying to prove to yourself and to others. Include in the list everything you need to be happy.

Based on what we have learned, God is 100% pleased with you. You have an eternal promise that you are everything he ever dreamed you would be.

Now here is your choice I continue to be enslaved to always pursuing, proving, building and all the pressure and frustration that comes along with it or accept Jesus and the freedom that comes with him being responsible to make me worthy, significant, beautiful, eternal. Then I am free to soak up all he has to give and free to give my life away to the ones I love. That is living by GRACE!!!!

Leaving Frustration Behind

Connect

- Welcome to 40 Days of Grace! Take just a few minutes for everyone to introduce themselves.

- Fill out the Life Group Covenant together.

- Opening Prayer:

Grow

Memory Verse:

But, now a righteousness from God, apart from the law to which the law and prophets testify. (Romans 3:21)

Have a Bible handy we will be studying Romans 1:16– 3:20.

**Watch the journaling portion of the DVD.
Use the next page to journal.**

SESSION 1

Journaling Question

*Is God 100% pleased with you?
If yes, why? If no, why not?*

SESSION 1

**Watch the lesson portion of the DVD
and follow along in your outline.**

Somehow we all know we are going to answer to God.

*(16) "I am not ashamed of the gospel, because it is the power of God
for the salvation of everyone who believes: first for the Jew, then for
the Gentile. (17) For in the gospel a righteousness from God is
revealed, a righteousness that is by faith from first to last, just as it is
written: "The righteous will live by faith.   (18) The wrath of God
is being revealed from heaven against all the godlessness and
wickedness of men who suppress the truth by their wickedness ..."*
(Romans 1:16-18)

1. I _____ care what God says –

I answer to _____, or something I made.

> *(28) "Furthermore, since they did not think it worthwhile to retain the
> knowledge of God, he gave them over to a depraved mind, to do what
> ought not to be done. (29)They have become filled with every kind of
> wickedness, evil, greed and depravity. They are full of envy, murder,
> strife, deceit and malice. They are gossips, (30) slanderers, God-haters,
> insolent, arrogant and boastful; they invent ways of doing evil; they
> disobey their parents; (31) they are senseless, faithless, heartless,
> ruthless. (32) Although they know God's righteous decree that those who
> do such things deserve death, they not only continue to do these very
> things but also approve of those who practice them."* (Romans 1:28-32)

SESSION 1

God's response– Just because you ignore me does not mean that I

will _____ you.

I am a _____. Look how much better I am than

him/her.

I answer to my _____.

> *(1)"You, therefore, have no excuse, you who pass judgment on someone else, for at whatever point you judge the other, you are condemning yourself, because you who pass judgment do the same things..."*
> (Romans 2:1)

God's response- You will be judged by how well you

_____ to your conscience.

> *"...since they show that the requirements of the law are written on their hearts, their consciences also bearing witness, and their thoughts now accusing, now even defending them. (16) This will take place on the day when God will judge men's secrets through Jesus Christ, as my gospel declares."*
> (Romans 2:15-16)

3. I know the _____, I am a spiritual person – I answer to

the _____.

SESSION 1

(17) "Now you, if you call yourself a Jew; if you rely on the law and brag about your relationship to God; (18) if you know his will and approve of what is superior because you are instructed by the law; (19) if you are convinced that you are a guide for the blind, a light for those who are in the dark, (20) an instructor of the foolish, a teacher of infants, because you have in the law the embodiment of knowledge and truth — (24) As it is written: 'God's name is blasphemed among the Gentiles because of you.' (Romans 2:17-20, 24)

God's response- You will not be judged by how much you
_____ or believe.

You will be judged upon _____ the law perfectly.

> *"Circumcision has value if you observe the law, but if you break the law, you have become as*
>   *though you had not been circumcised."* (Rom 2:25)

4. You don't have to tell me, I know I'm in _____ – I answer to God and there

is no _____!

"As it is written: 'There is no one righteous, not even one; (11) there is no one who understands, no one who seeks God. (12) All have turned away, they have together become worthless; there is no one who does good, not even one.'" (Romans 3:11-12)

God _____ him based on who a person is not just what they do.

What does the Bible say about answering to God?

_____trying to impress him by focusing on your own efforts.

*"Therefore no one will be declared righteous in his sight by observing the law; rather, through the law
  we become conscious of sin."* (Romans 3:20)

No one will be declared good, pure, right in his sight by observing the law because no one can be made right with God by following the law. The law only shows us our sin.

SESSION 1

Discussion Questions

1. If you're up to it, share the answer and percentage you gave to the beginning question, "Is God 100% pleased with me?"

2. What pressure is there in your life to become pleasing to others, God, parents, friends, boss, even yourself?

3. Is there anything a person can do to become pleasing to God, — anything they can change, produce or behave differently? Does becoming pleasing to God have anything to do with our behavior?

4. Now that you know following a code of behavior will not change your standing with God what are you going to start doing? What are you going to stop doing?

If you have enough time:

5. So after all of this, you're still going to answer to God — what can your heart hope in?

SESSION 1

Putting It Into Practice

Outreach

Choose an individual or family to love for the next 6 weeks.
Be creative and even a little crazy. Commit to pray for this
family each week through the 40 days.

Worship

Pray for each other that we open our hearts to what God
wants to for them over the 40 days.
Use 3 x 5 cards to write down your prayers as you come in
each week. Then pray over them later and at home during the
week.

SESSION 1

SESSION 1 – MESSAGE NOTES

Is God 100% pleased with you?

If yes, why?
If no please give a percentage, like I think God is 50 percent pleased with me.
Give the reason why you gave that percentage.

"For in the gospel a righteousness from God is revealed, a righteousness that is by faith from first to last, just as it is written: "The righteous will live by faith."

Rom 1:17

You be the judge. Watch these video clips, and then. YOU DECIDE...

1. **What would it take for you to ignore this person's attitude and actions and claim them acceptable, good, clean, righteous, praise worthy?**

   It would take...

2. **How much better than others would this person have to be for you to vouch for him or her, to look the other way and declare this person trustworthy with your heart, your child's heart, to let others know they can trust this person?**

   It would take...

3. What religion would this person have to be a part of for you to declare them pure, like God in character, one to be imitated or a representative of God?

    It would take...

God answers...

"Therefore no one will be declared righteous in his sight by observing the law; rather, through the law we become conscious of sin."

Rom 1:20

What is the first step to experiencing God's grace?

_____

_____

God is a _____ and _____ pure judge.

Controlling _____ does not change_____.

If this won't work, what am I going to do? How am I going to be OK, connected, whole, acceptable?
.

Questions? Send them to: **Grace@skylinenj.org**
I would love to hear them!

SESSION TWO

Opening God's Best

Connect

Share about a person with good character from your childhood or someone you know today that caused you to say, "I want to be like him/her."

Opening Prayer:

Grow

Memory Verse:

"This righteousness from God comes through faith in Jesus Christ to all who believe for there is no difference." (Romans 3:22)

Have a Bible handy we will be studying Romans 3:21-26.

 **Watch the journaling portion of the DVD.
Use the next page to journal.**

SESSION TWO

Journaling Question

*In any given moment, what do the
voices inside you say about you?*

Watch the lesson portion of the DVD and follow along in your outline.

(21) And now righteousness from God, apart from law, has been made known, to which the Law and the Prophets testify. (22) This righteousness from God comes through faith in Jesus Christ to all who believe. There is no difference, (23) for all have sinned and fall short of the glory of God, (24) and are justified freely by his grace through the redemption that came by Christ Jesus. (25) God presented him as a sacrifice of atonement, through faith in his blood. He did this to demonstrate his justice, because in his forbearance he had left sins committed beforehand unpunished – (26) he did it to demonstrate his justice at the present time, so as to be just and the one who justifies those who have faith in Jesus. (Romans 3:21-26)

1. How does God give his gifts?

_____

Through _____ in Jesus Christ

By His _____

SESSION TWO

"There is no difference, for all have sinned and fall short of the glory of God ..." (vs 23)

This means that you and I are qualified for grace because we have no goodness or value of our own.

2. What happens when God gives his goodness?

I am declared _____.

"... and are justified freely by his grace." (vs. 24)

All my debts are _____.

"... and are justified freely by his grace through the redemption that came by Christ Jesus (vs. 24)

God will never be _____ with me again.

3. What is life like if this is true?

I have nothing to _____.

SESSION TWO

"Who can say God's people are guilty? No one because Christ Jesus died, but he was also raised from the dead, and now he is on God's right side, appealing to God for us." (Romans 8:34)

I know exactly where I _____. I belong to Jesus.

"If we live, we live to the Lord; and if we die, we die to the Lord. So, whether we live or die, we belong to the Lord." (Romans 14:8)

I can go to God at any _____ about anything!

"For you did not receive a spirit that makes you a slave again to fear, but you received the Spirit of sonship. And by him we cry, "Abba, Father." (Romans 8:15)

SESSION TWO

Discussion Questions

1. What area of your life do you need God's grace or God's goodness?

2. Of all of the three things that happen when God gives us his goodness, which is your favorite and why?

3. How do you react when someone gives you a gift? Do you feel like you owe them something now?

4. With God offering so much why do people choose to say no?

5. How will it affect the way we treat and view each other if we have the same righteousness?

6. Does anyone want to share what they wrote during the journaling time?

7. What would have been a good question to ask at this point? Email it to **grace@skylinenj.org**.

SESSION TWO

8. What questions have come up in your group that need an answer? Email it to grace@skylinenj.org.

SESSION TWO

Putting It Into Practice

Serve

Adopt another Life Group to pour your grace out on. Come up with three ways to show grace to your adopted group. Set a date and time to accomplish one of your ideas.

Worship

Pray for the ones you are loving outside of Skyline.
Pray for the Life Group you have adopted.
Pray from the 3 x 5 cards.
Spend some time singing together if your group chooses.

SESSION TWO

SESSION TWO – MESSAGE NOTES

Opening the Box

"But now a righteousness from God, apart from law, has been made known, to which the Law and the Prophets testify. This righteousness from God comes through faith in Jesus Christ to all who believe. There is no difference, for all have sinned and fall short of the glory of God, and are justified freely by his grace through the redemption that came by Christ Jesus. God presented him as a sacrifice of atonement, through faith in his blood."

Romans 3:21-25

How do I gain access to God's goodness?

Through _____ in_____ _____ to all who_____.

Something amazing happens to all believers...

God _____ their evil and _____ it with his goodness.

This is word is called _____.

How?

Jesus _____the price I _____. This word is called _____.

Who did Jesus pay for?

Jesus _____ God's anger over my sin. This word is called _____.

What do I have to do?

God offers this to you for_____.

God offers this to you by_____.

You have to say

_____

_____

_____

_____.

SESSION THREE

Experimenting with Grace

Connect

Share about a time when you placed faith in someone or something. Did that person or that thing came through or fail you?

Opening Prayer:

Grow

Memory Verse:
"...for all have sinned and fall short of the glory of God." Romans 3:23

Have a Bible handy we will be studying Romans 5:12-14; 7:7-13; 4:16-23; 5:20-21

 **Watch the journaling portion of the DVD.
Use the next page to journal**

SESSION THREE

Journaling Question

*How do you feel when someone tells
you not to do something?*

Watch the lesson portion of the DVD and follow along in your outline.

1. **Principle of "The Sin" and Death**

We don't die just because of _____ we do. It's

because of _____ we are.

(11) Therefore, just as sin entered the world through one man, and death through sin, and in the same way death came to all men, because all sinned – (13) for before the law was given, sin was in the world. But sin is not taken into account when there is no law. (14)Nevertheless, death reigned from the time of Adam to the time of Moses, even over those who did not sin by breaking a command, as did Adam, who was a pattern of the one to come ".(Romans 5:12-14)

SESSION THREE

2. Principle of Sin and the Law

(7) "What shall we say then? Is the law sin? Certainly not! Indeed I would not have known what sin was except through the law. For I would not have known what coveting really was if the law had not said, "Do not covet." (8) But sin, seizing the opportunity afforded by the commandment, produced in me every kind of covetous desire. For apart from the law, Sin is dead.(9) Once I was alive apart from the law; but when the commandment came, sin sprang to life and I died. (10) I found that the very commandment that was intended to bring life actually brought death." (Romans 7:7-10)

A. We became _____ to "The Sin"

   Clarification: "The Sin" vs. Acts of Sin

(9) "Once I was alive apart from the law; but when the commandment came, sin sprang to life and I died." (Romans 7:9)

B. The more God _____ me about his will the more I _____ it.

SESSION THREE

C. "The Sin" is dead or powerless without the

_____.

3. Principle of law and transgression

If there is not law our sins are not _____ down

Clarification: Transgressions = Acts of Sin

How do I gain access to God's grace?

By: _____

(18) "Against all hope, Abraham in hope believed and so became the father of many nations, just as it had been said to him, "So shall your offspring be."(19) Without weakening in his faith, he faced the fact that his body was as good as dead – since he was about a hundred years old – and that Sarah's womb was also dead. (20) Yet he did not waver through unbelief regarding the promise of God, but was strengthened in his faith and gave glory to God. (21) being fully persuaded that God had power to do what he had promised. (22) This is why "it was credited to him as righteousness." (Romans 4:18-22)

SESSION THREE

1. Face the _____.

2. Face the _____ or word of God.

3. _____ to believe what God says (to believe is to act upon what God says).

How do I get God's grace?

4. Principle of Sin and Grace

"The law was added so that the trespass might increase, but where sin increased, grace increased all the more! So that just as sin reigned in death, so also grace might reign through righteousness to bring eternal life through Jesus Christ our Lord." (Romans 5:20-21)

The more I _____ the more grace I get.

SESSION THREE

Discussion Questions:

1. Does anyone want to share their answer to the journaling question?

2. What are the 3 components of Biblical faith? Are you practicing faith in God if you don't have all three?

3. According to the book of Romans, why does the law exist?

4. If it is true that "the more I sin the more grace I get," what do you think God is going to do once you've sinned?

5. Share your plan to get more of God's grace this week.

6. Email your questions to grace@skylinenj.org.

SESSION THREE

Putting It Into Practice

Share

Review your plan to love someone outside of Skyline. How is it going? Work together to carry out your plans or make new ones and carry those out.

Worship

Pray over your 3 x 5 cards
Pray for your adopted group
Sing

SESSION THREE

Experimenting with Grace

What is faith in Jesus Christ? Is it...

    1. _____

    2. _____

    3. What I _____ it to be

1. _____ the facts.

2. _____ God's promise.

3. _____ your faith in one or the other.

"Yet he did not waver through unbelief regarding the promise of God, but was strengthened in his faith and gave glory to God, being fully persuaded that God had power to do what he had promised."
                         Romans 4:20-21

God has promised me... _____, to make me a

new_____, and to pay for

all of my_____.

Where is your faith?

Let's practice!

SESSION THREE – MESSAGE NOTES

1. Because God has made me _____, I have

_____with God.

2. I stand in _____.

"The law was added so that the trespass might increase. But where sin increased, grace increased all the more, so that, just as sin reigned in death, so also grace might reign through righteousness to bring eternal life through Jesus Christ our Lord."

Romans 5:20-21

"Against all hope, Abraham in hope believed and so became the father of many nations, just as it had been said to him, "So shall your offspring be." Without weakening in his faith, he faced the fact that his body was as good as dead – since he was about a hundred years old – and that Sarah's womb was also dead. Yet he did not waver through unbelief regarding the promise of God, but was strengthened in his faith and gave glory to God, being fully persuaded that God had power to do what he had promised. This is why "it was credited to him as righteousness." The words "it was credited to him" were written not for him alone, but also for us, to whom God will credit righteousness – for us who believe in him who raised Jesus our Lord from the dead. He was delivered over to death for our sins and was raised to life for our justification."

Romans 4:18-25

"Therefore, since we have been justified through faith, we have peace with God through our Lord Jesus Christ, through whom we have gained access by faith into this grace in which we now stand."

Romans 5:1-2

SESSION FOUR

Staying Outside the Box

Connect

Share the most effective things your parents or other adults did to make you behave.

Share the most ineffective ways your they tried to make you behave.

Opening Prayer:

Grow

Memory Verse:

"And are justified freely by his grace through the redemption that came by Jesus Christ."
(Romans 3:24)

Have a Bible handy we will be studying Romans 6.

 **Watch the journaling portion of the DVD.
Use the next page to journal**

SESSION FOUR

Journaling Question

*If someone were to give you a fresh start on life,
how would you live your life?*

Watch the lesson portion of the DVD and follow along in your outline.

Why not sin?
Because that's not _____ I am.

1. I have a new _____.
   a. I died.

"What shall we say then? Shall we go on sinning so grace may increase? By no means! We died to sin.
For we know that our old self was crucified with him so that the body of sin might be done away with, that we should no longer be slaves to sin." (Romans 6:1&6, 7)

   b. I'm _____. I have a new direction, a new purpose.

"The death he died, he died to sin once for all; but the life he lives, he lives to God. In the same way, count yourselves dead to sin but alive to God in Jesus Christ. (Romans 6: 10-11)

   c. My _____ belongs to God so now live out who you are.

"Do not offer the parts of your body to sin, as instruments of wickedness, but rather offer yourselves to God, as those who have been brought from death to life; and offer the parts of your body to him as instruments of righteousness. (Romans 6:13)

SESSION FOUR

2. Sin is no longer my _____. The box is gone.

   "For sin shall not be your master, because you are no longer under law, but under grace."
   (Romans 6: 14)

3. If I am not going to pay for the sin, why not keep on sinning?

   a. Because that is not _____ I am.

   "You have been set free from sin and have become slaves to righteousness." (Romans 6:18)

   b. There is no _____ from sin. It only causes hurt and destroys.

   "What benefit did you reap at that time from the things you are now ashamed of? Those things result in death!" (Romans 6: 21)

   c. Because sin leads to death and following Christ leads to life.

   "But now that you have been set free from sin and have become slaves to God, the benefit you reap leads to holiness, and the result is eternal life." (Romans 6:22)

SESSION FOUR

Discussion Questions

Does anyone want to share what they wrote in their
   journaling question?

2. What motivation have you used in the past to stop sinning?

3. What reasons does Paul give for not sinning?

4. Once you're under God's grace, who are you?

5. What are the walls of your box made out of?

6. Now that you know the box doesn't exist how do you feel?
How do you feel knowing your box has disappeared?

7. What keeps you from trusting what God says about you?

E-mail your questions to grace@skylinenj.org

SESSION FOUR

Staying Outside the Box

Putting It Into Practice

Ministry

Plan a fun night for after the 40 Days.
How is your adopted group doing? Review your plans to love
them and keep up the good work.

Worship

Pray for the 3 x 5 cards
Next week we will be sharing the Lord's   Supper
Sing together using the DVD

SESSION FOUR

Living Outside of The Box

"What shall we say, then? Shall we go on sinning so that grace may increase?
Shall we continue in sin?"

Romans 6:1

What do you use as your motivation not to sin?

Guilt, _____, Bribery, _____, Begging, _____

What does Paul say is the reason not to sin?

That is not _____.

      a. I _____.

"...We died to sin; how can we live in it any longer?"

Romans 6:2

"For we know that our old self was crucified with him so that the body of sin might be done away with, that we should no longer be slaves to sin."

Romans 6:6

      The person who was a slave to sin _____!

      b. I am _____.

      The person I am now lives _____for God!

      c. I live under _____.

"For sin shall not be your master because you're not under law, but under grace."

Romans 6:14

"Sin is not taken into account when there is no law"

Romans 5:13

There is no _____!

If I will never pay for the sin, then why not sin?

1. Because that is not _____.

"But thanks be to God, that you wholeheartedly obeyed the form of teaching to which you were entrusted. You have been set free from sin and have become slaves to righteousness."

Romans 6:18

2. Nothing _____ comes from sin.

SESSION FIVE

Gracefully Changing From the Inside Out

Connect

If you have tried it, share what it is like living without the box.

Share an area of your life where you have had personal victory … an area where others say you have changed for the better or share an area of your life you would like to change.

Grow

Memory Verse:

"God presented him as a sacrifice of atonement, through faith in his blood. He did this to demonstrate his justice because in his forbearance he had left the sins committed before hand unpunished." (Romans 3:25)

Have a Bible handy we will be studying Romans 7:14 – 8:17

 **Watch the journaling portion of the DVD.
Use the next page to journal**

SESSION FIVE

Journaling Question

What keeps me from doing who I really am?

**Watch the lesson portion of the DVD
and follow along in your outline.**

*"For what I do is not the good I want to do; no, the evil I do not
want to do — this I keep on doing. 20 Now if I do what I do not
want to do, it is no longer I who do it, but sin living in me that does
it.*
(Romans 7:19-20)

Why do I still sin?
How do I get to where I want to go?

*(21) So I find this law at work: When I want to do good, evil is right
there with me. (22) For in the inner being I delight in God's law;
(23) but I see another law at work in the members of my body,
waging war against the law of my mind and making me a prisoner of
the law of sin at work within my members.*
 *(24) What a wretched man I am! Who will rescue me from this
body of death? (25) Thanks be to God — through Jesus Christ our
Lord! So then, I myself in my mind am a slave to God's law, but in
the sinful nature a slave to the law of sin. (8:1) Therefore, there is
now no condemnation to those who are in Christ Jesus".*
(Romans 7:21-8:1)

SESSION FIVE

(6) "The mind of sinful man is death, but the mind controlled by the Spirit is life and peace; (7) the sinful mind is hostile to God. It does not submit to God's law, nor can it do so. (8) so those controlled by the sinful nature cannot please God. (Romans 8:6-8)

3 Major Players Involved:

1. _____/Flesh

2. You/Your _____

3. _____Spirit

How do I overcome the flesh?

2 Key Phrases:

1. To live in the new way of the Spirit.
   To live in the new way of the Spirit simply means I listen to God's Spirit and do
   what he says.

2. Put to _____ the deeds of the flesh by the Spirit.

How do I put to death the deeds of the flesh by the Spirit?

1. _____ that my flesh is wretched.

2. _____ what God has said is true about me.

3. Put the _____ to death.

4. By Repenting and Replacing

   • Repenting is an act.
   • Exposing the sin to God and then to others
   • Turning away
   • Replace with a God activity

SESSION FIVE

Discussion Questions

1. Does anyone want to share what they wrote in their journaling question?

2. Who is a believer in Christ's worst enemy?

3. How does our flesh or sin nature bring pain and frustration into our lives?

4. The description of wretched seems really strong. Do you agree or disagree and why?

5. What does God think of us while we are wrestling with sin, failure, temptation?

6. Using what we have learned today, what would you tell a believer who cannot stop cursing?

SESSION FIVE

Putting It Into Practice

 Use the Lord's Supper DVD

Worship

Put on the Lord's Supper DVD and have a great time thanking Jesus for all he has done for you

Staying Outside Of The Box!

Is God pleased with me?

1. I am in trouble because of _____ I am and what I have done.

2. God _____ me by grace His goodness by paying for who I am and what I have done.

3. I can _____ by placing my faith in Jesus Christ.

4. He _____ me in a new relationship of grace. The more sin the more grace.

5. The reason not to sin is because of _____ I am.

6. I am dead to sin, _____to God like Jesus, under grace.

So if all of this is true why do I still sin?

I sin because of the incredible _____ within.

"So I find this law (principle) at work: When I want to do good, evil is right there with me. For in my inner being I delight in God's law; but I see another law (principle) at work in the members of my body, waging war against the law (principle) of my mind and making me a prisoner of the law (principle) of sin at work within my members. What a wretched man I am! Who will rescue me from this body of death? Thanks be to God – through Jesus Christ our Lord! So then, I myself in my mind am a slave to God's law, but in the sinful nature a slave to the law (principle) of sin."

Romans 7:21-25

There are two sides...

On the one side is my spirit and God's spirit. I _____ God's law. (vs 22)

On the other side is my _____, and Satan. It is driven to live under the law. (vs 23)

SESSION FIVE – MESSAGE NOTES

The war is not over the choice to _____ or do good, to serve or do nothing, to tell the _____ or lie.

At any given moment the war is over _____ I am. (vs 23)

What am I under? Law or _____? (vs 25)

"What shall we say, then? Is the law sin? Certainly not! Indeed I would not have known what sin was except through the law. For I would not have known what coveting really was if the law had not said, "Do not covet." But sin, seizing the opportunity afforded by the commandment, produced in me every kind of covetous desire. For apart from law, sin is dead. Once I was alive apart from law; but when the commandment came, sin sprang to life and I died. I found that the very commandment that was intended to bring life actually brought death.

For sin, seizing the opportunity afforded by the commandment, deceived me, and through the commandment put me to death. So then, the law is holy, and the commandment is holy, righteous and good. Did that which is good, then, become death to me? By no means! But in order that sin might be recognized as sin, it produced death in me through what was good, so that through the commandment sin might become utterly sinful."

Romans 7:7-13

If I am under grace then I am a slave to _____ and live by the _____.

If I am under law then I am a slave to _____ and live by the _____.

SESSION FIVE – MESSAGE NOTES

So who does God say that I am?

I am a _____ of Jesus Christ

who belongs to everyone else at

Skyline Community Church!

"...so in Christ we who are many form one body, and each member belongs to all the others. We have different gifts, according to the grace given us. If a man's gift is prophesying, let him use it in proportion to his faith."

Romans 12:5,6

SESSION SIX

Celebrating Changed Lives

Connect

What in the world is God doing? Share your perspective on
what God is up to in our world?

Grow

Memory Verse:

*"He did it to demonstrate his justice at the present time, so as to be just
and the one who justifies those who have faith in Jesus."* (Romans 3:26)

Have a Bible handy we will be studying Romans 8:28-39

 **Watch the journaling portion of the DVD.
Use the next page to journal**

SESSION SIX

Journaling Question

*If you knew someone loved you unconditionally,
how would you live your life?*

Watch the lesson portion of the DVD and follow along in your outline.

What is God doing in my life right now?

Changing me from the _____ out

    1. Using every thing that happens in my life to

    _____ me be more Christ

      like.

    "We know that in everything God works for the good of those who love him. They are the people he called, because that was his plan." (Romans 8: 28)

    2. He is _____ me.

(33) "Who will bring any charge against those whom God has chosen? It is God who justifies. (34) Who is he that condemns? Jesus Christ, who died – more than that, who was raised to life – is at the right hand of God and is also interceding for us. (Romans 8: 33-34)

SESSION SIX

3. _____ me.

(35) "Who shall separate us from the love of Christ? Shall trouble or hardship or persecution or famine or nakedness or danger or sword? (36) As it is written: "For your sake we face death all day long; for we are considered as sheep to be slaughtered." (37) No, in all these things we are more than conquerors through him who loved us. (38) I am convinced that neither death nor life; neither angels nor demons, neither the present nor the future, nor any powers, neither height nor depth, nor anything else in all creation, will be able to separate us from the love of God that is in Christ Jesus our Lord. (Romans 8: 35-38)

SESSION SIX

"Therefore, I urge you, brothers, in view of God's mercy, to offer your bodies as living sacrifices, holy and pleasing to God– this is your spiritual act of worship."   (Romans 12:1)

4. He is telling me the _____.

"Do not conform any longer to the pattern of this world, but be transformed by the renewing of your mind. Then you will be able to test and approve what God's will is – his good, pleasing and perfect will." (Romans 12:2)

5. He is using me to form his body which is where I

_____.

"Just as each of us has one body with many members, and these members do not all have the same functions, so in Christ we who are many form one body, and each member belongs to all of the others."
  (Romans 12:4)

SESSION SIX

Celebrating Changed Lives

Discussion Questions

1. Does anyone want to share what they wrote during the journaling time?

2. What are some practical things that would change about you if your were like Christ on the outside?

3. How does knowing that God is using everything for my own good, impact the way we react to bad circumstances?

4. When do you feel separated from God's love?

5. According to what we have learned about grace is there ever a time when God is disappointed with you?

6. Over the past 6 weeks what has God been changing in you?

7. Describe what it means to experience God's grace from what we have learned in Romans?

Email questions to grace@skylinenj.org

SESSION SIX

Putting It Into Practice

Serve

Plan a fun night for your group some time in the next 3 weeks.
Plan what you want to share at the Celebration Dinner about
God's grace in your life.

Worship

Pray using the requests on the 3 x5 cards

SESSION SIX

You're either Becoming More like Christ or You're Headed Back to the Box!

"And we know that in all things God works for the good of those who love him, who have been called according to his purpose. For those God foreknew he also predestined to be conformed to the likeness of his Son."

Romans 8:28-29

Two questions...

1. How do I get out of this mess with the least amount of change possible?

2. How do you want to use this to make me more like you?

"No, in all these things we are more than conquerors through him who loved us. For I am convinced that neither death nor life, neither angels nor demons, neither the present nor the future, nor any powers, neither height nor depth, nor anything else in all creation, will be able to separate us from the love of God that is in Christ Jesus our Lord."

Romans 8:37-39

What do our circumstances tell us about God's love?

FINAL SESSION – MESSAGE NOTES

Grasping the New Life God Offers

"Therefore, I urge you, brothers, in view of God's mercy, to offer your bodies as living sacrifices, holy and pleasing to God – this is your spiritual act of worship."

Romans 12:1

I will live a life of hope, love, encouragement and strength when I...

1. _____His Grace.

"No, in all these things we are more than conquerors through him who loved us."

Romans 8:37

2. _____ with Sacrifice.

      A. I do it _____and in my every day _____.

"Then he said to them all: "If anyone would come after me, he must deny himself and take up his cross daily and follow me."

Matthew 16:24

B. I give him _____ _____ or _____ _____ and

I give him _____ ___ _____

.

"If anyone comes to me and does not hate his father and mother, his wife and children, his brothers and sisters – yes, even his own life – he cannot be my disciple."

Luke 14:26

C. I give it out of _____ in him, His word and His _____ for me.

"For the kingdom of God is not a matter of eating and drinking, but of righteousness, peace and joy in the Holy Spirit, because anyone who serves Christ in this way is pleasing to God and approved by men."

Romans 14:17-18

Made in the USA
San Bernardino, CA
20 January 2016